PENGUIN BOOK

We Will All Go Down F...

Winston Churchill

1874–1965

Winston Churchill

*We Will All Go Down
Fighting to the End*

PENGUIN BOOKS — GREAT IDEAS

PENGUIN BOOKS

Published by the Penguin Group

Penguin Books Ltd, 80 Strand, London wc2r 0rl, England

Penguin Group (USA) Inc., 375 Hudson Street, New York, New York 10014, USA

Penguin Group (Canada), 90 Eglinton Avenue East, Suite 700, Toronto, Ontario, Canada m4p 2y3
(a division of Pearson Penguin Canada Inc.)

Penguin Ireland, 25 St Stephen's Green, Dublin 2, Ireland (a division of Penguin Books Ltd)

Penguin Group (Australia), 250 Camberwell Road, Camberwell, Victoria 3124, Australia
(a division of Pearson Australia Group Pty Ltd)

Penguin Books India Pvt Ltd, 11 Community Centre, Panchsheel Park, New Delhi – 110 017, India

Penguin Group (NZ), 67 Apollo Drive, Rosedale, North Shore 0632, New Zealand
(a division of Pearson New Zealand Ltd)

Penguin Books (South Africa) (Pty) Ltd, 24 Sturdee Avenue, Rosebank, Johannesburg 2196,
South Africa

Penguin Books Ltd, Registered Offices: 80 Strand, London wc2r 0rl, England

www.penguin.com

This selection published in Penguin Books 2010

007

Speeches copyright © The Estate of Winston Churchill

Set in 11/13 Dante MT Std
Typeset by TexTech International
Printed in England by Clays Ltd, St Ives plc

ISBN: 978-0-141-19253-6

www.greenpenguin.co.uk

MIX
Paper from
responsible sources
FSC™ C018179

Penguin Books is committed to a sustainable
future for our business, our readers and our planet.
This book is made from Forest Stewardship
Council™ certified paper.

Contents

'A total and unmitigated defeat'

5 October 1938

House of Commons

In the general euphoria that greeted Chamberlain's handling of the Munich Conference, Churchill's speech attacking appeasement seemed at the time entirely inappropriate.

If I do not begin this afternoon by paying the usual, and indeed almost invariable, tributes to the Prime Minister for his handling of this crisis, it is certainly not from any lack of personal regard. We have always, over a great many years, had very pleasant relations, and I have deeply understood from personal experiences of my own in a similar crisis the stress and strain he has had to bear; but I am sure it is much better to say exactly what we think about public affairs, and this is certainly not the time when it is worth anyone's while to court political popularity. We had a shining example of firmness of character from the late First Lord of the Admiralty two days ago. He showed that firmness of character which is utterly unmoved by currents of opinion, however swift and violent they may be. My hon. Friend the Member for South-West Hull (Mr Law), to whose compulsive speech the House listened on Monday – which I had not the good fortune to hear, but which I read, and which I am assured by all who heard it revived the memory of his famous father, so cherished in this House, and made us feel that his gifts did not die with him – was quite right in reminding us that the Prime Minister has himself throughout his conduct of these matters shown a robust indifference to cheers or boos and to the alternations of criticism and applause. If that be so, such qualities and elevation of mind should make it possible for the most severe expressions of honest opinion to be interchanged in this House without rupturing personal relations, and for all points of view to receive the fullest possible expression.

Having thus fortified myself by the example of others, I will proceed to emulate them. I will, therefore, begin by saying the most unpopular and most unwelcome thing. I will begin by saying what everybody would like to ignore or forget but which must nevertheless be stated, namely, that we have sustained a total and unmitigated defeat, and that France has suffered even more than we have.

Viscountess Astor: Nonsense.

Mr Churchill: When the Noble Lady cries 'Nonsense', she could not have heard the Chancellor of the Exchequer [Sir John Simon] admit in his illuminating and comprehensive speech just now that Herr Hitler had gained in this particular leap forward in substance all he set out to gain. The utmost my right hon. Friend the Prime Minister has been able to secure by all his immense exertions, by all the great efforts and mobilizations which took place in this country, and by all the anguish and strain through which we have passed in this country, the utmost he has been able to gain – [*Hon. Members*: 'Is peace.'] I thought I might be allowed to make that point in its due place, and I propose to deal with it. The utmost he has been able to gain for Czechoslovakia and in the matters which were in dispute has been that the German dictator, instead of snatching his victuals from the table, has been content to have them served to him course by course.

The Chancellor of the Exchequer said it was the first time Herr Hitler had been made to retract – I think that was the word – in any degree. We really must not waste time, after all this long debate, upon the difference between the positions reached at Berchtesgaden, at Godesberg and at Munich. They can be very simply epitomized, if the House will permit me to vary the metaphor. £1 was demanded at the pistol's point. When it was given, £2 were demanded at the pistol's point. Finally, the dictator consented to take £1 17s. 6d. and the rest in promises of goodwill for the future.

Now I come to the point, which was mentioned to me just now from some quarters of the House, about the saving of peace. No one has been a more resolute and uncompromising struggler for peace than the Prime Minister. Everyone knows that. Never has there been such intense and undaunted determination to maintain and to secure peace. That is quite true. Nevertheless, I am not quite clear why there was so much danger of Great Britain or France being involved in a war with Germany at this juncture if, in fact, they were ready all along to sacrifice Czechoslovakia. The terms which the Prime Minister brought back with him – I quite agree at the last moment; everything had got off the rails and nothing but his intervention could have saved the peace, but I am talking of the events of the summer – could easily have been agreed, I believe, through the ordinary diplomatic channels at any time during the summer. And I will say this, that I believe the Czechs, left to themselves and told they were going to get no help from the Western Powers, would have been able to make better terms than they have got – they could hardly have worse – after all this tremendous perturbation.

There never can be any absolute certainty that there will be a fight if one side is determined that it will give way completely. When one reads the Munich terms, when one sees what is happening in Czechoslovakia from hour to hour, when one is sure, I will not say of Parliamentary approval but of Parliamentary acquiescence, when the Chancellor of the Exchequer makes a speech which at any rate tries to put in a very powerful and persuasive manner the fact that, after all, it was inevitable and indeed righteous – right – when we saw all this, and everyone on this side of the House, including many Members of the Conservative Party who are supposed to be vigilant and careful guardians of the national interest, it is quite clear that nothing vitally affecting us was at stake, it seems to me that one must ask, What was all the trouble and fuss about?

The resolve was taken by the British and the French Governments. Let me say that it is very important to realize that it is by no means a question which the British Government only have had to decide. I very much admire the manner in which, in the House, all references of a recriminatory nature have been repressed, but it must be realized that this resolve did not emanate particularly from one or other of the Governments but was a resolve for which both must share in common the responsibility. When this resolve was taken and the course was followed – you may say it was wise or unwise, prudent or short-sighted – once it had been decided not to make the defence of Czechoslovakia a matter of war, then there was really no reason, if the matter had been handled during the summer in the ordinary way, to call into being all this formidable apparatus of crisis. I think that point should be considered.

We are asked to vote for this Motion ['That this House approves the policy of His Majesty's Government by which war was averted in the recent crisis and supports their efforts to secure a lasting peace'] which has been put upon the Paper, and it is certainly a Motion couched in very uncontroversial terms, as, indeed, is the Amendment moved from the Opposition side. I cannot myself express my agreement with the steps which have been taken and, as the Chancellor of the Exchequer has put his side of the case with so much ability I will attempt, if I may be permitted, to put the case from a different angle. I have always held the view that the maintenance of peace depends upon the accumulation of deterrents against the aggressor, coupled with a sincere effort to redress grievances. Herr Hitler's victory, like so many of the famous struggles that have governed the fate of the world, was won upon the narrowest of margins. After the seizure of Austria in March we faced this problem in our Debates. I ventured to appeal to the Government to go a little further than the Prime Minister went, and to give a pledge that in conjunction with France and other Powers they would guarantee the security of Czechoslovakia while the Sudeten-Deutsch question was being examined either by a League of Nations Commission or some other impartial body, and I still believe that if that course had been followed events would not have fallen into this disastrous state. I agree very much with my right hon. Friend the Member for Sparkbrook (Mr Amery) when he said on that occasion – I cannot remember his actual words – 'Do one thing or the other: either say you will disinterest yourself in the matter altogether or take the step of giving a guarantee which will have the greatest chance of securing protection for that country.'

France and Great Britain together, especially if they had maintained a close contact with Russia, which certainly was not done, would have been able in those days in the summer, when they had the prestige, to influence many of the smaller States of Europe, and I believe they could have determined the attitude of Poland. Such a combination, prepared at a time when the German dictator was not deeply and irrevocably committed to his new adventure, would, I believe, have given strength to all those forces in Germany which resisted this departure, this new design. They were varying forces, those of a military character which declared that Germany was not ready to undertake a world war, and all that mass of moderate opinion and popular opinion which dreaded war, and some elements of which still have some influence upon the German Government. Such action would have given strength to all that intense desire for peace which the helpless German masses share with their British and French fellow men, and which, as we have been reminded, found a passionate and rarely permitted vent in the joyous manifestations with which the Prime Minister was acclaimed in Munich.

All these forces, added to the other deterrents which combinations of Powers, great and small, ready to stand firm upon the front of law and for the ordered remedy of grievances, would have formed, might well have been effective. Of course you cannot say for certain that they would. [*Interruption.*] I try to argue fairly with the House. At the same time I do not think it is fair to charge those who wished to see this course followed, and followed consistently and resolutely, with having wished for an immediate war. Between submission and immediate war there was this third alternative, which gave a hope not only of peace but of justice. It is quite true that such a policy in order to succeed demanded that Britain should declare straight out and a long time beforehand that she would, with others, join to defend Czechoslovakia against an unprovoked aggression. His Majesty's Government refused to give that guarantee when it would have saved the situation, yet in the end they gave it when it was too late, and now, for the future, they renew it when they have not the slightest power to make it good.

All is over. Silent, mournful, abandoned, broken, Czechoslovakia recedes into the darkness. She has suffered in every respect by her association with the Western democracies and with the League of Nations, of which she has always been an obedient servant. She has suffered in particular from her association with France, under whose guidance and policy she has been actuated for so long. The very measures taken by His Majesty's Government in the Anglo-French Agreement to give her the best chance possible, namely, the 50 per cent clean-cut in certain districts instead of a plebiscite, have turned to her detriment,

7

because there is to be a plebiscite, too, in wide areas, and those other Powers who had claims have also come down upon the helpless victim. Those municipal elections upon whose voting the basis is taken for the 50 per cent cut were held on issues which had nothing to do with joining Germany. When I saw Herr Henlein over here he assured me that was not the desire of his people. Positive statements were made that it was only a question of home rule, of having a position of their own in the Czechoslovakian State. No one has a right to say that the plebiscite which is to be taken in areas under Saar conditions, and the clean-cut of the 50 per cent areas – that those two operations together amount to the slightest degree to a verdict of self-determination. It is a fraud and a farce to invoke that name.

We in this country, as in other Liberal and democratic countries, have a perfect right to exalt the principle of self-determination, but it comes ill out of the mouths of those in totalitarian States who deny even the smallest element of toleration to every section and creed within their bounds. But, however you put it, this particular block of land, this mass of human beings to be handed over, has never expressed the desire to go into the Nazi rule. I do not believe that even now – if their opinion could be asked – they would exercise such an option.

What is the remaining position of Czechoslovakia? Not only are they politically mutilated, but, economically and financially, they are in complete confusion. Their banking, their railway arrangements, are severed and broken, their industries are curtailed, and the movement of their population is most cruel. The Sudeten miners, who are all

Czechs and whose families have lived in that area for centuries, must now flee into an area where there are hardly any mines left for them to work. It is a tragedy which has occurred. I did not like to hear the Minister of Transport yesterday talking about Humpty Dumpty. It was the Minister of Transport who was saying that it was a case of Humpty Dumpty that could never be put together again. There must always be the most profound regret and a sense of vexation in British hearts at the treatment and the misfortunes which have overcome the Czechoslovakian Republic. They have not ended here. At any moment there may be a hitch in the programme. At any moment there may be an order for Herr Goebbels to start again his propaganda of calumny and lies; at any moment an incident may be provoked, and now that the fortress line is given away what is there to stop the will of the conqueror? [*Interruption.*] It is too serious a subject to treat lightly. Obviously, we are not in a position to give them the slightest help at the present time, except what everyone is glad to know has been done, the financial aid which the Government have promptly produced.

I venture to think that in future the Czechoslovak State cannot be maintained as an independent entity. You will find that in a period of time which may be measured by years, but may be measured only by months, Czechoslovakia will be engulfed in the Nazi régime. Perhaps they may join it in despair or in revenge. At any rate, that story is over and told. But we cannot consider the abandonment and ruin of Czechoslovakia in the light only of what happened only last month. It is the most grievous consequence which we have yet experienced of what we have done and of what we have left undone in the last five years – five years of futile good intention, five years of eager search started for the line of least resistance, five years of uninterrupted retreat of British power, five years of neglect of our air defences. Those are the features which I stand here to declare and which marked an improvident stewardship for which Great Britain and France have dearly to pay. We have been reduced in those five years from a position of security so overwhelming and so unchallengeable that we never cared to think about it. We have been reduced from a position where the very word 'war' was considered one which would be used only by persons qualifying for a lunatic asylum. We have been reduced from a position of safety and power – power to do good, power to be generous to a beaten foe, power to make terms with Germany, power to give her proper redress for her grievances, power to stop her arming if we chose, power to take any step in strength or mercy or justice which we thought right – reduced in five years from a position safe and unchallenged to where we stand now.

When I think of the fair hopes of a long peace which still lay before Europe at the beginning of 1933 when Herr Hitler first obtained power, and of all the opportunities of arresting the growth of the Nazi power which have been thrown away, when I think of the immense combinations and resources which have been neglected or squandered, I cannot believe that a parallel exists in the whole course of history. So far as this country is concerned the responsibility must rest with those who have the undisputed control of our political affairs. They neither prevented Germany from rearming, nor did they rearm ourselves in time. They quarrelled with Italy without saving Ethiopia. They exploited and discredited the vast institution of the League of Nations and they neglected to make alliances and combinations which might have repaired previous errors, and thus they left us in the hour of trial without adequate national defence or effective international security.

In my holiday I thought it was a chance to study the reign of King Ethelred the Unready. The House will remember that that was a period of great misfortune, in which, from the strong position which we had gained under the descendants of King Alfred, we fell very swiftly into chaos. It was the period of Danegeld and of foreign pressure. I must say that the rugged words of the *Anglo-Saxon Chronicle*, written 1,000 years ago, seem to me apposite, at least as apposite as those quotations from Shakespeare with which we have been regaled by the last speaker from the Opposition Bench. Here is what the *Anglo-Saxon Chronicle* said, and I think the words apply very much to our treatment of Germany and our relations with her:

> All these calamities fell upon us because of evil counsel, because tribute was not offered to them at the right time nor yet were they resisted; but when they had done the most evil, then was peace made with them.

That is the wisdom of the past, for all wisdom is not new wisdom.

I have ventured to express those views in justifying

myself for not being able to support the Motion which is moved tonight, but I recognize that this great matter of Czechoslovakia, and of British and French duty there, has passed into history. New developments may come along, but we are not here to decide whether any of those steps should be taken or not. They have been taken. They have been taken by those who had a right to take them because they bore the highest executive responsibility under the Crown. Whatever we may think of it, we must regard those steps as belonging to the category of affairs which are settled beyond recall. The past is no more, and one can only draw comfort if one feels that one has done one's best to advise rightly and wisely and in good time. I, therefore, turn to the future, and to our situation as it is today. Here, again, I am sure I shall have to say something which will not be at all welcome.

We are in the presence of a disaster of the first magnitude which has befallen Great Britain and France. Do not let us blind ourselves to that. It must now be accepted that all the countries of Central and Eastern Europe will make the best terms they can with the triumphant Nazi Power. The system of alliances in Central Europe upon which France has relied for her safety has been swept away, and I can see no means by which it can be reconstituted. The road down the Danube Valley to the Black Sea, the resources of corn and oil, the road which leads as far as Turkey, has been opened. In fact, if not in form, it seems to me that all those countries of Middle Europe, all those Danubian countries, will, one after another, be drawn into this vast system of power politics – not only power military politics but power economic politics – radiating from Berlin, and I believe this can be achieved quite smoothly and swiftly and will not necessarily entail the firing of a single shot . . .

You will see, day after day, week after week, entire alienation of those regions. Many of those countries, in fear of the rise of the Nazi Power, have already got politicians, Ministers, Governments, who were pro-German, but there was always an enormous popular movement in Poland, Rumania, Bulgaria and Yugoslavia which looked to the Western democracies and loathed the idea of having this arbitrary rule of the totalitarian system thrust upon them, and hoped that a stand would be made. All that has gone by the board. We are talking about countries which are a long way off and of which, as the Prime Minister might say, we know nothing. [*Interruption.*] The noble Lady says that that very harmless allusion is –

Viscountess Astor: Rude.

Mr Churchill: She must very recently have been receiving her finishing course in manners. What will be the position, I want to know, of France and England this year and the year afterwards? What will be the position of that Western front of which we are in full authority the guarantors? The German army at the present time is more numerous than that of France, though not nearly so matured or perfected. Next year it will grow much larger, and its maturity will be more complete. Relieved from all anxiety in the East, and having secured resources which will greatly diminish, if not entirely remove, the deterrent of a naval blockade, the rulers of Nazi Germany will have a free choice open to them in what direction they will turn their eyes. If the Nazi dictator should choose to look westward, as he may, bitterly will France and England regret the loss of that fine army of ancient Bohemia which was estimated last week to require not fewer than 30 German divisions for its destruction.

Can we blind ourselves to the great change which has taken place in the military situation, and to the dangers we have to meet? We are in process, I believe, of adding, in four years, four battalions to the British Army. No fewer than two have already been completed. Here are at least 30 divisions which must now be taken into consideration upon the French front, besides the 12 that were captured when Austria was engulfed. Many people, no doubt, honestly believe that they are only giving away the interests of Czechoslovakia, whereas I fear we shall find that we have deeply compromised, and perhaps fatally endangered, the safety and even the independence of Great Britain and France. This is not merely a question of giving up the German colonies, as I am sure we shall be asked to do. Nor is it a question only of losing influence in Europe. It goes far deeper than that. You have to consider the character of the Nazi movement and the rule which it implies. The Prime Minister desires to see cordial relations between this country and Germany. There is no difficulty at all in having cordial relations with the German people. Our hearts go out to them. But they have no power. You must have diplomatic and correct relations, but there can never be friendship between the British democracy and the Nazi Power, that Power which spurns Christian ethics, which cheers its onward course by a barbarous paganism, which vaunts the spirit of aggression and conquest, which derives strength and perverted pleasure from persecution, and uses, as we have seen, with pitiless brutality the threat of murderous force. That Power cannot ever be the trusted friend of the British democracy.

What I find unendurable is the sense of our country falling into the power, into the orbit and influence of Nazi Germany, and of our existence becoming dependent upon their goodwill or pleasure. It is to prevent that that I have tried my best to urge the maintenance of every bulwark of defence – first the timely creation of an Air Force superior to anything within striking distance of our shores; secondly, the gathering together of the collective strength of many nations; and thirdly, the making of alliances and military conventions, all within the Covenant, in order to gather together forces at any rate to restrain the onward movement of this Power. It has all been in vain. Every position has been successively undermined and abandoned on specious and plausible excuses. We do not want to be led upon the high road to becoming a satellite of the German Nazi system of European domination. In a very few years, perhaps in a very few months, we shall be confronted with demands with which we shall no doubt be invited to comply. Those demands may affect the surrender of territory or the surrender of liberty. I foresee and foretell that the policy of submission will carry with it restrictions upon the freedom of speech and debate in Parliament, on public platforms, and discussions in the Press, for it will be said – indeed, I hear it said sometimes now – that we cannot allow the Nazi system of dictatorship to be criticized by ordinary, common English politicians. Then, with a Press under control, in part direct but more potently indirect, with every organ of public opinion doped and chloroformed into acquiescence, we shall be conducted along further stages of our journey. . . .

I have been casting about to see how measures can be taken to protect us from this advance of the Nazi Power, and to secure those forms of life which are so dear to us. What is the sole method that is open? The sole method that is open is for us to regain our old island independence by acquiring that supremacy in the air which we were promised, that security in our air defences which we were assured we had, and thus to make ourselves an island once again. That, in all this grim outlook, shines out as the overwhelming fact. An effort at rearmament the like of which has not been seen ought to be made forthwith, and all the resources of this country and all its united strength should be bent to that task. I was very glad to see that Lord Baldwin yesterday in the House of Lords said that he would mobilize industry tomorrow. But I think it would have been much better if Lord Baldwin had said that 2½ years ago, when everyone demanded a Ministry of Supply. I will venture to say to hon. Gentlemen sitting here behind the Government Bench, hon. Friends of mine, whom I thank for the patience with which they have listened to what I have to say, that they have some responsibility for all this too, because, if they had given one tithe of the cheers they have lavished upon this transaction of Czechoslovakia to the small band of Members who were endeavouring to get timely rearmament set in motion, we should not now be in the position in which we are. Hon. Gentlemen opposite, and hon. Members on the Liberal benches, are not entitled to throw these stones. I remember for two years having to face, not only the Government's deprecation, but their stern disapproval. Lord Baldwin has now given the signal, tardy though it may be; let us at least obey it.

After all, there are no secrets now about what happened in the air and in the mobilization of our anti-aircraft defences. These matters have been, as my hon. and gallant Friend the Member for the Abbey Division said, seen by thousands of people. They can form their own opinions of the character of the statements which have been persistently made to us by Ministers on this subject. Who pretends now that there is air parity with Germany? Who pretends now that our anti-aircraft defences were adequately manned or armed? We know that the German General Staff are well informed upon these subjects, but the House of Commons has hitherto not taken seriously its duty of requiring to assure itself on these matters. The Home Secretary [Sir Samuel Hoare] said the other night that he would welcome investigation. Many things have been done which reflect the greatest credit upon the administration. But the vital matters are what we want to know about. I have asked again and again during these three years for a secret Session where these matters could be thrashed out, or for an investigation by a Select Committee of the House, or for some other method. I ask now that, when we meet again in the autumn, that should be a matter on which the Government should take the House into its confidence, because we have a right to know where we stand and what measures are being taken to secure our position.

I do not grudge our loyal, brave people, who were ready to do their duty no matter what the cost, who never flinched under the strain of last week – I do not grudge them the natural, spontaneous outburst of joy and relief when they learned that the hard ordeal would no longer be required of them at the moment; but they should know the truth. They should know that there has been gross neglect and deficiency in our defences; they should know that we have sustained a defeat without a war, the consequences of which will travel far with us along our road; they should know that we have passed an awful milestone in our history, when the whole equilibrium of Europe has been deranged, and that the terrible words have for the time being been pronounced against the Western democracies:

'Thou art weighed in the balance and found wanting.'

And do not suppose that this is the end. This is only the beginning of the reckoning. This is only the first sip, the first foretaste of a bitter cup which will be proffered to us year by year unless, by a supreme recovery of moral health and martial vigour, we arise again and take our stand for freedom as in the olden time.

War

3 September 1939

House of Commons

Churchill's first speech following Chamberlain's announcement earlier on the same day that Britain was at war with Nazi Germany.

In this solemn hour it is a consolation to recall and to dwell upon our repeated efforts for peace. All have been ill-starred, but all have been faithful and sincere. This is of the highest moral value – and not only moral value, but practical value – at the present time, because the wholehearted concurrence of scores of millions of men and women, whose co-operation is indispensable and whose comradeship and brotherhood are indispensable, is the only foundation upon which the trial and tribulation of modern war can be endured and surmounted. This moral conviction alone affords that ever-fresh resilience which renews the strength and energy of people in long, doubtful and dark days. Outside, the storms of war may blow and the lands may be lashed with the fury of its gales, but in our own hearts this Sunday morning there is peace. Our hands may be active, but our consciences are at rest.

We must not underrate the gravity of the task which lies before us or the temerity of the ordeal, to which we shall not be found unequal. We must expect many disappointments, and many unpleasant surprises, but we may be sure that the task which we have freely accepted is one not beyond the compass and the strength of the British Empire and the French Republic. The Prime Minister said it was a sad day, and that is indeed true, but at the present time there is another note which may be present, and that is a feeling of thankfulness that, if these great trials were to come upon our Island, there is a generation of Britons here now ready to prove itself not unworthy of the days of yore and not unworthy of those great men, the fathers of our land, who laid the foundations of our laws and shaped the greatness of our country.

This is not a question of fighting for Danzig or fighting for Poland. We are fighting to save the whole world from the pestilence of Nazi tyranny and in defence of all that is most sacred to man. This is no war of domination or imperial aggrandizement or material gain; no war to shut any country out of its sunlight and means of progress. It is a war, viewed in its inherent quality, to establish, on impregnable rocks, the rights of the individual, and it is a war to establish and revive the stature of man. Perhaps it might seem a paradox that a war undertaken in the name of liberty and right should require, as a necessary part of its processes, the surrender for the time being of so many of the dearly valued liberties and rights. In these last few days the House of Commons has been voting dozens of Bills which hand over to the executive our most dearly valued traditional liberties. We are sure that these liberties will be in hands which will not abuse them, which will use them for no class or party interests, which will cherish and guard them, and we look forward to the day, surely and confidently we look forward to the day, when our liberties and rights will be restored to us, and when we shall be able to share them with the peoples to whom such blessings are unknown.

'Blood, toil, tears and sweat'

13 May 1940

House of Commons

Following Chamberlain's resignation, Churchill became Prime Minister on 10 May. He gave this extraordinary speech to rally support to his new government and in response to the increasingly alarming news from Europe.

I beg to move,

That this House welcomes the formation of a Government representing the united and inflexible resolve of the nation to prosecute the war with Germany to a victorious conclusion.

On Friday evening last I received His Majesty's Commission to form a new Administration. It was the evident wish and will of Parliament and the nation that this should be conceived on the broadest possible basis and that it should include all parties, both those who supported the late Government and also the parties of the Opposition. I have completed the most important part of this task. A War Cabinet has been formed of five Members, representing, with the Opposition Liberals, the unity of the nation. The three party Leaders have agreed to serve, either in the War Cabinet or in high executive office. The three Fighting Services have been filled. It was necessary that this should be done in one single day, on account of the extreme urgency and rigour of events. A number of other positions, key positions, were filled yesterday, and I am submitting a further list to His Majesty tonight. I hope to complete the appointment of the principal Ministers during tomorrow. The appointment of the other Ministers usually takes a little longer, but I trust that, when Parliament meets again, this part of my task will be completed, and that the administration will be complete in all respects.

I considered it in the public interest to suggest that the House should be summoned to meet today. Mr Speaker agreed, and took the necessary steps, in accordance with the powers conferred upon him by the Resolution of the House. At the end of the proceedings today, the Adjournment of the House will be proposed until Tuesday, 21 May, with, of course, provision for earlier meeting, if need be. The business to be considered during that week will be notified to Members at the earliest opportunity. I now invite the House, by the Motion which stands in my name, to record its approval of the steps taken and to declare its confidence in the new Government.

To form an Administration of this scale and complexity is a serious undertaking in itself, but it must be remembered that we are in the preliminary stage of one of the greatest battles in history, that we are in action at many other points in Norway and in Holland, that we have to be prepared in the Mediterranean, that the air battle is continuous and that many preparations, such as have been indicated by my hon. Friend below the Gangway, have to be made here at home. In this crisis I hope I may be pardoned if I do not address the House at any length today. I hope that any of my friends and colleagues, or former colleagues, who are affected by the political reconstruction, will make allowance, all allowance, for any lack of ceremony with which it has been necessary to act. I would say to the House, as I said to those who have joined this Government: 'I have nothing to offer but blood, toil, tears and sweat.'

We have before us an ordeal of the most grievous kind. We have before us many, many long months of struggle and of suffering. You ask, what is our policy? I can say: It is to wage war, by sea, land and air, with all our might and with all the strength that God can give us; to wage war against a monstrous tyranny, never surpassed in the dark, lamentable catalogue of human crime. That is our policy. You ask, what is our aim? I can answer in one word: It is victory, victory at all costs, victory in spite of all terror, victory, however long and hard the road may be; for without victory, there is no survival. Let that be realized; no survival for the British Empire, no survival for all that the British Empire has stood for, no survival for the urge and impulse of the ages, that mankind will move forward towards its goal. But I take up my task with buoyancy and hope. I feel sure that our cause will not be suffered to fail among men. At this time I feel entitled to claim the aid of all, and I say, 'Come then, let us go forward together with our united strength.'

'Arm yourselves, and be ye men of valour!'

19 May 1940

Broadcast, London

Churchill's first radio broadcast as Prime Minister, made as it became clear that the Anglo-French forces were facing total defeat.

I speak to you for the first time as Prime Minister in a solemn hour for the life of our country, of our Empire, of our Allies, and, above all, of the cause of Freedom. A tremendous battle is raging in France and Flanders. The Germans, by a remarkable combination of air bombing and heavily armoured tanks, have broken through the French defences north of the Maginot Line, and strong columns of their armoured vehicles are ravaging the open country, which for the first day or two was without defenders. They have penetrated deeply and spread alarm and confusion in their track. Behind them there are now appearing infantry in lorries, and behind them, again, the large masses are moving forward. The re-groupment of the French armies to make head against, and also to strike at, this intruding wedge has been proceeding for several days, largely assisted by the magnificent efforts of the Royal Air Force.

We must not allow ourselves to be intimidated by the presence of these armoured vehicles in unexpected places behind our lines. If they are behind our Front, the French are also at many points fighting actively behind theirs. Both sides are therefore in an extremely dangerous position. And if the French Army, and our own Army, are well handled, as I believe they will be; if the French retain that genius for recovery and counter-attack for which they have so long been famous; and if the British Army shows the dogged endurance and solid fighting power of which there have been so many examples in the past – then a sudden transformation of the scene might spring into being.

It would be foolish, however, to disguise the gravity of the hour. It would be still more foolish to lose heart and courage or to suppose that well-trained, well-equipped armies numbering three or four millions of men can be overcome in the space of a few weeks, or even months, by a scoop, or raid of mechanized vehicles, however formidable. We may look with confidence to the stabilization of the Front in France, and to the general engagement of the masses, which will enable the qualities of the French and British soldiers to be matched squarely against those of their adversaries. For myself, I have invincible confidence in the French Army and its leaders. Only a very small part of that splendid Army has yet been heavily engaged; and only a very small part of France has yet been invaded. There is good evidence to show that practically the whole of the specialized and mechanized forces of the enemy have been already thrown into the battle; and we know that very heavy losses have been inflicted upon them. No officer or man, no brigade or division, which grapples at close quarters with the enemy, wherever encountered, can fail to make a worthy contribution to the general result. The Armies must cast away the idea of resisting behind concrete lines or natural obstacles, and must realize that mastery can only be regained by furious and unrelenting assault. And this spirit must not only animate the High Command, but must inspire every fighting man.

In the air – often at serious odds, often at odds hitherto thought overwhelming – we have been clawing down three or four to one of our enemies; and the relative balance of the British and German Air Forces is now considerably more favourable to us than at the beginning of the battle. In cutting down the German bombers we are fighting our own battle as well as that of France. My confidence in our ability to fight it out to the finish with the German Air Force has been strengthened by the fierce encounters which have taken place and are taking place. At the same time, our heavy bombers are striking nightly at the tap-root of German mechanized power, and have already inflicted serious damage upon the oil refineries on which the Nazi effort to dominate the world directly depends.

We must expect that as soon as stability is reached on the Western Front, the bulk of that hideous apparatus of aggression which gashed Holland into ruin and slavery in a few days will be turned upon us. I am sure I speak for all when I say we are ready to face it; to endure it; and to retaliate against it – to any extent that the unwritten laws of war permit. There will be many men and many women in this Island who when the ordeal comes upon them, as come it will, will feel comfort, and even a pride, that they are sharing the perils of our lads at the Front – soldiers, sailors and airmen, God bless them – and are drawing away from them a part at least of the onslaught they have to bear. Is not this the appointed time for all to make the utmost exertions in their power? If the battle is to be won, we must provide our men with ever-increasing quantities of the weapons and ammunition they need. We must have, and have quickly, more aeroplanes, more tanks, more shells, more guns. There is imperious need for these vital munitions. They increase our strength against the powerfully armed enemy. They replace the wastage of the obstinate struggle; and the knowledge that wastage will speedily be replaced enables us to draw more readily upon our reserves and throw them in now that everything counts so much.

Our task is not only to win the battle – but to win the war. After this battle in France abates its force, there will come the battle for our Island – for all that Britain is, and all that Britain means. That will be the struggle. In that supreme emergency we shall not hesitate to take every step, even the most drastic, to call forth from our people the last ounce and the last inch of effort of which they are capable. The interests of property, the hours of labour, are nothing compared with the struggle of life and honour, for right and freedom, to which we have vowed ourselves.

I have received from the Chiefs of the French Republic, and in particular from its indomitable Prime Minister, M. Reynaud, the most sacred pledges that whatever happens they will fight to the end, be it bitter or be it glorious. Nay, if we fight to the end, it can only be glorious.

Having received His Majesty's commission, I have formed an Administration of men and women of every Party and of almost every point of view. We have differed and quarrelled in the past; but now one bond unites us all – to wage war until victory is won, and never to surrender ourselves to servitude and shame, whatever the cost and the agony may be. This is one of the most awe-striking periods in the long history of France and Britain. It is also beyond doubt the most sublime. Side by side, unaided except by their kith and kin in the great Dominions and by the wide Empires which rest beneath their shield – side by side, the British and French peoples have advanced to rescue not only Europe but mankind from the foulest and most soul-destroying tyranny which has ever darkened and stained the pages of history. Behind them – behind us – behind the Armies and Fleets of Britain and France – gather a group of shattered States and bludgeoned races: the Czechs, the Poles, the Norwegians, the Danes, the Dutch, the Belgians – upon all of whom the long night of barbarism will descend, unbroken even by a star of hope, unless we conquer, as conquer we must; as conquer we shall.

Today is Trinity Sunday. Centuries ago words were written to be a call and a spur to the faithful servants of Truth and Justice: 'Arm yourselves, and be ye men of valour, and be in readiness for the conflict; for it is better for us to perish in battle than to look upon the outrage of our nation and our altar. As the Will of God is in Heaven, even so let it be.'

'Wars are not won by evacuations'

4 June 1940

House of Commons

Churchill reports on the sequence of events that led to the successful evacuation of Dunkirk.

From the moment that the French defences at Sedan and on the Meuse were broken at the end of the second week of May, only a rapid retreat to Amiens and the south could have saved the British and French Armies who had entered Belgium at the appeal of the Belgian King; but this strategic fact was not immediately realized. The French High Command hoped they would be able to close the gap, and the Armies of the north were under their orders. Moreover, a retirement of this kind would have involved almost certainly the destruction of the fine Belgian Army of over 20 divisions and the abandonment of the whole of Belgium. Therefore, when the force and scope of the German penetration were realized and when a new French Generalissimo, General Weygand, assumed command in place of General Gamelin, an effort was made by the French and British Armies in Belgium to keep on holding the right hand of the Belgians and to give their own right hand to a newly created French Army

which was to have advanced across the Somme in great
strength to grasp it.

However, the German eruption swept like a sharp
scythe around the right and rear of the Armies of the
north. Eight or nine armoured divisions, each of about
four hundred armoured vehicles of different kinds, but
carefully assorted to be complementary and divisible into
small self-contained units, cut off all communications
between us and the main French Armies. It severed our
own communications for food and ammunition, which
ran first to Amiens and afterwards through Abbeville,
and it shore its way up the coast to Boulogne and Calais,
and almost to Dunkirk. Behind this armoured and mechanized onslaught came a number of German divisions in
lorries, and behind them again there plodded compara-
tively slowly the dull brute mass of the ordinary German
Army and German people, always so ready to be led to
the trampling down in other lands of liberties and com-
forts which they have never known in their own.

I have said this armoured scythe-stroke almost reached
Dunkirk – almost but not quite. Boulogne and Calais were
the scenes of desperate fighting. The Guards defended
Boulogne for a while and were then withdrawn by orders
from this country. The Rifle Brigade, the 60th Rifles, and
the Queen Victoria's Rifles, with a battalion of British
tanks and 1,000 Frenchmen, in all about four thousand
strong, defended Calais to the last. The British Brigadier
was given an hour to surrender. He spurned the offer,
and four days of intense street fighting passed before
silence reigned over Calais, which marked the end of a
memorable resistance. Only 30 unwounded survivors

were brought off by the Navy, and we do not know the fate of their comrades. Their sacrifice, however, was not in vain. At least two armoured divisions, which otherwise would have been turned against the British Expeditionary Force, had to be sent to overcome them. They have added another page to the glories of the light division, and the time gained enabled the Gravelines waterlines to be flooded and to be held by the French troops.

Thus it was that the port of Dunkirk was kept open. When it was found impossible for the Armies of the north to reopen their communications to Amiens with the main French Armies, only one choice remained. It seemed, indeed, forlorn. The Belgian, British and French Armies were almost surrounded. Their sole line of retreat was to a single port and to its neighbouring beaches. They were pressed on every side by heavy attacks and far outnumbered in the air.

When, a week ago today, I asked the House to fix this afternoon as the occasion for a statement, I feared it would be my hard lot to announce the greatest military disaster in our long history. I thought – and some good judges agreed with me – that perhaps 20,000 or 30,000 men might be re-embarked. But it certainly seemed that the whole of the French First Army and the whole of the British Expeditionary Force north of the Amiens–Abbeville gap would be broken up in the open field or else would have to capitulate for lack of food and ammunition. These were the hard and heavy tidings for which I called upon the House and the nation to prepare themselves a week ago. The whole root and core and brain of the British

Army, on which and around which we were to build, and are to build, the great British Armies in the later years of the war, seemed about to perish upon the field or to be led into an ignominious and starving captivity.

That was the prospect a week ago. But another blow which might well have proved final was yet to fall upon us. The King of the Belgians had called upon us to come to his aid. Had not this Ruler and his Government severed themselves from the Allies, who rescued their country from extinction in the late war, and had they not sought refuge in what was proved to be a fatal neutrality, the French and British Armies might well at the outset have saved not only Belgium but perhaps even Poland. Yet at the last moment, when Belgium was already invaded, King Leopold called upon us to come to his aid, and even at the last moment we came. He and his brave, efficient Army, nearly half a million strong, guarded our left flank and thus kept open our only line of retreat to the sea. Suddenly, without prior consultation, with the least possible notice, without the advice of his Ministers and upon his own personal act, he sent a plenipotentiary to the German Command, surrendered his Army, and exposed our whole flank and means of retreat.

I asked the House a week ago to suspend its judgment because the facts were not clear, but I do not feel that any reason now exists why we should not form our own opinions upon this pitiful episode. The surrender of the Belgian Army compelled the British at the shortest notice to cover a flank to the sea more than 30 miles in length. Otherwise all would have been cut off, and all would have shared the fate to which King Leopold had condemned the finest Army his country had ever formed. So in doing this and in exposing this flank, as anyone who followed the operations on the map will see, contact was lost between the British and two out of the three corps forming the First French Army, who were still farther from the coast than we were, and it seemed impossible that any large number of Allied troops could reach the coast.

The enemy attacked on all sides with great strength and fierceness, and their main power, the power of their far more numerous Air Force, was thrown into the battle or else concentrated upon Dunkirk and the beaches. Pressing in upon the narrow exit, both from the east and from the west, the enemy began to fire with cannon upon the beaches by which alone the shipping could approach or depart. They sowed magnetic mines in the channels and seas; they sent repeated waves of hostile aircraft, sometimes more than a hundred strong in one formation, to cast their bombs upon the single pier that remained, and upon the sand dunes upon which the troops had their eyes for shelter. Their U-boats, one of which was sunk, and their motor launches took their toll of the vast traffic which now began. For four or five days an intense struggle reigned. All their armoured divisions – or what was left of them – together with great masses of infantry and artillery, hurled themselves in vain upon the ever-narrowing, ever-contracting appendix within which the British and French Armies fought.

Meanwhile, the Royal Navy, with the willing help of countless merchant seamen, strained every nerve to embark the British and Allied troops; 220 light warships and 650 other vessels were engaged. They had to operate upon the difficult coast, often in adverse weather, under an almost ceaseless hail of bombs and an increasing concentration of artillery fire. Nor were the seas, as I have said, themselves free from mines and torpedoes. It was in conditions such as these that our men carried on, with little or no rest, for days and nights on end, making trip after trip across the dangerous waters, bringing with them always men whom they had rescued. The numbers they have brought back are the measure of their devotion and their courage. The hospital ships, which brought off many thousands of British and French wounded, being so plainly marked were a special target for Nazi bombs; but the men and women on board them never faltered in their duty.

Meanwhile, the Royal Air Force, which had already been intervening in the battle, so far as its range would allow, from home bases, now used part of its main metropolitan fighter strength, and struck at the German bombers and at the fighters which in large numbers protected them. This struggle was protracted and fierce. Suddenly the scene has cleared, the crash and thunder has for the moment – but only for the moment – died away. A miracle of deliverance, achieved by valour, by perseverance, by perfect discipline, by faultless service, by resource, by skill, by unconquerable fidelity, is manifest to us all. The enemy was hurled back by the retreating British and French troops. He was so roughly handled that he did not harry their departure seriously. The Royal Air Force engaged the main strength of the German Air Force, and inflicted upon them losses of at least four to one; and the Navy, using nearly 1,100 ships of all kinds, carried over 335,000 men, French and British, out of the jaws of death and shame, to their native land and to the tasks which lie immediately ahead. We must be very careful not to assign to this deliverance the attributes of a victory. Wars are not won by evacuations. But there was a victory inside this deliverance, which should be noted. It was gained by the Air Force. Many of our soldiers coming back have not seen the Air Force at work; they saw only the bombers which escaped its protective attack. They underrate its achievements. I have heard much talk of this; that is why I go out of my way to say this. I will tell you about it.

This was a great trial of strength between the British and German Air Forces. Can you conceive a greater objective for the Germans in the air than to make evacuation from these beaches impossible, and to sink all these ships which were displayed, almost to the extent of thousands? Could there have been an objective of greater military importance and significance for the whole purpose of the war than this? They tried hard, and they were beaten back; they were frustrated in their task. We got the Army away; and they have paid fourfold for any losses which they have inflicted. Very large formations of German aeroplanes – and we know that they are a very brave race – have turned on several occasions from the attack of one-quarter of their number of the Royal Air Force, and have dispersed in different directions. Twelve aeroplanes have been hunted by two. One aeroplane was driven into the water and cast away by the mere charge of a British aeroplane, which had no more ammunition.

All of our types – the Hurricane, the Spitfire and the new Defiant – and all our pilots have been vindicated as superior to what they have at present to face.

When we consider how much greater would be our advantage in defending the air above this Island against an overseas attack, I must say that I find in these facts a sure basis upon which practical and reassuring thoughts may rest. I will pay my tribute to these young airmen. The great French Army was very largely, for the time being, cast back and disturbed by the onrush of a few thousands of armoured vehicles. May it not also be that the cause of civilization itself will be defended by the skill and devotion of a few thousand airmen? There never has been, I suppose, in all the world, in all the history of war, such an opportunity for youth. The Knights of the Round Table, the Crusaders, all fall back into the past – not only distant but prosaic; these young men, going forth every morn to guard their native land and all that we stand for, holding in their hands these instruments of colossal and shattering power, of whom it may be said that

> Every morn brought forth a noble chance
> And every chance brought forth a noble knight,

deserve our gratitude, as do all the brave men who, in so many ways and on so many occasions, are ready, and continue ready to give life and all for their native land.

I return to the Army. In the long series of very fierce battles, now on this front, now on that, fighting on three fronts at once, battles fought by two or three divisions against an unequal or somewhat larger number of the enemy, and fought fiercely on some of the old grounds that so many of us knew so well – in these battles our losses in men have exceeded 30,000 killed, wounded and missing. I take occasion to express the sympathy of the House to all who have suffered bereavement or who are still anxious. The President of the Board of Trade [Sir Andrew Duncan] is not here today. His son has been killed, and many in the House have felt the pangs of affliction in the sharpest form. But I will say this about the missing: We have had a large number of wounded come home safely to this country, but I would say about the missing that there may be very many reported missing who will come back home, some day, in one way or another. In the confusion of this fight it is inevitable that many have been left in positions where honour required no further resistance from them.

Against the loss of over 30,000 men, we can set a far heavier loss certainly inflicted upon the enemy. But our losses in material are enormous. We have perhaps lost one-third of the men we lost in the opening days of the battle of 21 March, 1918, but we have lost nearly as many guns – nearly one thousand – and all our transport, all the armoured vehicles that were with the Army in the north. This loss will impose a further delay on the expansion of our military strength. That expansion had not been proceeding as far as we had hoped. The best of all we had to give had gone to the British Expeditionary Force, and although they had not the numbers of tanks and some articles of equipment which were desirable, they were a very well and finely equipped Army. They had the first fruits of all that our industry had to give, and that is gone.

And now here is this further delay. How long it will be, how long it will last, depends upon the exertions which we make in this Island. An effort the like of which has never been seen in our records is now being made. Work is proceeding everywhere, night and day, Sundays and week days. Capital and Labour have cast aside their interests, rights and customs and put them into the common stock. Already the flow of munitions has leaped forward. There is no reason why we should not in a few months overtake the sudden and serious loss that has come upon us, without retarding the development of our general programme.

Nevertheless, our thankfulness at the escape of our Army and so many men, whose loved ones have passed through an agonizing week, must not blind us to the fact that what has happened in France and Belgium is a colossal military disaster. The French Army has been weakened, the Belgian Army has been lost, a large part of those fortified lines upon which so much faith had been reposed is gone, many valuable mining districts and factories have passed into the enemy's possession, the whole of the Channel ports are in his hands, with all the tragic consequences that follow from that, and we must expect another blow to be struck almost immediately at us or at France. We are told that Herr Hitler has a plan for invading the British Isles. This has often been thought of before. When Napoleon lay at Boulogne for a year with his flat-bottomed boats and his Grand Army, he was told by someone. 'There are bitter weeds in England.' There are certainly a great many more of them since the British Expeditionary Force returned.

The whole question of home defence against invasion is, of course, powerfully affected by the fact that we have for the time being in this Island incomparably more powerful military forces than we have ever had at any moment in this war or the last. But this will not continue. We shall not be content with a defensive war. We have our duty to our Ally. We have to reconstitute and build up the British Expeditionary Force once again, under its gallant Commander-in-Chief, Lord Gort. All this is in train; but in the interval we must put our defences in this Island into such a high state of organization that the fewest possible numbers will be required to give effective security and that the largest possible potential of offensive effort may be realized. On this we are now engaged. It will be very convenient, if it be the desire of the House, to enter upon this subject in a secret Session. Not that the government would necessarily be able to reveal in very great detail military secrets, but we like to have our discussions free, without the restraint imposed by the fact that they will be read the next day by the enemy; and the Government would benefit by views freely expressed in all parts of the House by Members with their knowledge of so many different parts of the country. I understand that some request is to be made upon this subject, which will be readily acceded to by His Majesty's Government.

We have found it necessary to take measures of increasing stringency, not only against enemy aliens and suspicious characters of other nationalities, but also against British subjects who may become a danger or a nuisance should the war be transported to the United Kingdom. I know there are a great many people affected by the orders which we have made who are the passionate enemies of Nazi Germany. I am very sorry for them, but we cannot, at the present time and under the present stress, draw all the distinctions which we should like to do. If parachute landings were attempted and fierce fighting attendant upon them followed, these unfortunate people would be far better out of the way, for their own sakes as well as for ours. There is, however, another class, for which I feel not the slightest sympathy. Parliament has given us the powers to put down Fifth Column activities with a strong hand, and we shall use those powers subject to the supervision and correction of the House, without the slightest hesitation until we are satisfied, and more than satisfied, that this malignancy in our midst has been effectively stamped out.

Turning once again, and this time more generally, to the question of invasion, I would observe that there has never been a period in all these long centuries of which we boast when an absolute guarantee against invasion, still less against serious raids, could have been given to our people. In the days of Napoleon the same wind which would have carried his transports across the Channel might have driven away the blockading fleet. There was always the chance, and it is that chance which has excited and befooled the imaginations of many Continental tyrants. Many are the tales that are told. We are assured that novel methods will be adopted, and when we see the originality of malice, the ingenuity of aggression, which our enemy displays, we may certainly prepare ourselves for every kind of novel stratagem and every kind of brutal and treacherous manoeuvre. I think that no idea is so outlandish that it should not be considered and viewed with a searching, but at the same time, I hope, with a steady eye. We must never forget the solid assurances of sea power and those which belong to air power if it can be locally exercised.

I have, myself, full confidence that if all do their duty, if nothing is neglected, and if the best arrangements are made, as they are being made, we shall prove ourselves once again able to defend our Island home, to ride out the storm of war, and to outlive the menace of tyranny, if necessary for years, if necessary alone. At any rate, that is what we are going to try to do. That is the resolve of His Majesty's Government – every man of them. That is the will of Parliament and the nation. The British Empire and the French Republic, linked together in their cause and in their need, will defend to the death their native soil, aiding each other like good comrades to the utmost of their strength. Even though large tracts of Europe and many old and famous States have fallen or may fall into the grip of the Gestapo and all the odious apparatus of Nazi rule, we shall not flag or fail. We shall go on to the end, we shall fight in France, we shall fight on the seas and oceans, we shall fight with growing confidence and growing strength in the air, we shall defend our Island, whatever the cost may be, we shall fight on the beaches, we shall fight on the landing grounds, we shall fight in the fields and in the streets, we shall fight in the hills; we shall never surrender, and even if, which I do not for a moment believe, this Island or a large part of it were sub-jugated and starving, then our Empire beyond the seas, armed and guarded by the British Fleet, would carry on the struggle, until, in God's good time, the New World, with all its power and might, steps forth to the rescue and the liberation of the old.

'The Few'

20 August 1940

House of Commons

Churchill's response to the course of the Battle of Britain and tour d'horizon of the military situation in the summer of 1940.

Almost a year has passed since the war began, and it is natural for us, I think, to pause on our journey at this milestone and survey the dark, wide field. It is also useful to compare the first year of this second war against German aggression with its forerunner a quarter of a century ago. Although this war is in fact only a continuation of the last, very great differences in its character are apparent. In the last war millions of men fought by hurling enormous masses of steel at one another. 'Men and shells' was the cry, and prodigious slaughter was the consequence. In this war nothing of this kind has yet appeared. It is a conflict of strategy, of organization, of technical apparatus, of science, mechanics and morale. The British casualties in the first 12 months of the Great War amounted to 365,000. In this war, I am thankful to say, British killed, wounded, prisoners and missing, including civilians, do not exceed 92,000, and of these a large proportion are alive as prisoners of war. Looking more widely around, one may say that throughout all Europe, for one man killed or wounded in the first year perhaps five were killed or wounded in 1914–15.

The slaughter is only a small fraction, but the consequences to the belligerents have been even more deadly. We have seen great countries with powerful armies dashed out of coherent existence in a few weeks. We have seen the French Republic and the renowned French Army beaten into complete and total submission with less than the casualties which they suffered in any one of half a dozen of the battles of 1914–18. The entire body – it might almost seem at times the soul – of France has succumbed to physical effects incomparably less terrible than those which were sustained with fortitude and undaunted will-power 25 years ago. Although up to the present the loss of life has been mercifully diminished, the decisions reached in the course of the struggle are even more profound upon the fate of nations than anything that has ever happened since barbaric times. Moves are made upon the scientific and strategic boards, advantages are gained by mechanical means, as a result of which scores of millions of men become incapable of further resistance, or judge themselves incapable of further resistance, and a fearful game of chess proceeds from check to mate by which the unhappy players seem to be inexorably bound.

There is another more obvious difference from 1914. The whole of the warring nations are engaged, not only soldiers, but the entire population, men, women and children. The fronts are everywhere. The trenches are dug in the towns and streets. Every village is fortified. Every road is barred. The front line runs through the factories. The workmen are soldiers with different weapons but the same courage. These are great and distinctive changes from what many of us saw in the struggle of a quarter of a century ago. There seems to be every reason to believe that this new kind of war is well suited to the genius and the resources of the British nation and the British Empire; and that, once we get properly equipped and properly started, a war of this kind will be more favourable to us than the sombre mass slaughters of the Somme and Passchendaele. If it is a case of the whole nation fighting and suffering together, that ought to suit us, because we are the most united of all the nations, because we entered the war upon the national will and with our eyes open, and because we have been nurtured in freedom and individual responsibility and are the products, not of totalitarian uniformity, but of tolerance and variety. If all these qualities are turned, as they are being turned, to the arts of war, we may be able to show the enemy quite a lot of things that they have not thought of yet. Since the Germans drove the Jews out and lowered their technical standards, our science is definitely ahead of theirs. Our geographical position, the command of the sea and the friendship of the United States enable us to draw resources from the whole world and to manufacture weapons of war of every kind, but especially of the superfine kinds, on a scale hitherto practised only by Nazi Germany.

Hitler is now sprawled over Europe. Our offensive springs are being slowly compressed, and we must resolutely and methodically prepare ourselves for the campaigns of 1941 and 1942. Two or three years are not a long time, even in our short, precarious lives. They are nothing in the history of the nation, and when we are doing the finest thing in the world, and have the honour to be the sole champion of the liberties of all Europe, we must not grudge these years or weary as we toil and struggle through them. It does not follow that our energies in future years will be exclusively confined to defending ourselves and our possessions. Many opportunities may lie open to amphibious power, and we must be ready to take advantage of them. One of the ways to bring this war to a speedy end is to convince the enemy, not by words, but by deeds, that we have both the will and the means, not only to go on indefinitely, but to strike heavy and unexpected blows. The road to victory may not be so long as we expect. But we have no right to count upon this. Be it long or short, rough or smooth, we mean to reach our journey's end.

It is our intention to maintain and enforce a strict blockade, not only of Germany, but of Italy, France, and all the other countries that have fallen into the German power. I read in the papers that Herr Hitler has also proclaimed a strict blockade of the British Islands. No one can complain of that. I remember the Kaiser doing it in the last war. What indeed would be a matter of general complaint would be if we were to prolong the agony of all Europe by allowing food to come in to nourish the Nazis and aid their war effort, or to allow food to go in to the subjugated peoples, which certainly would be pillaged off them by their Nazi conquerors.

There have been many proposals, founded on the highest motives, that food should be allowed to pass the blockade for the relief of these populations. I regret that we must refuse these requests. The Nazis declare that they have created a new unified economy in Europe. They have repeatedly stated that they possess ample reserves of food and that they can feed their captive peoples. In a German broadcast of 27th June it was said that while Mr Hoover's plan for relieving France, Belgium and Holland deserved commendation, the German forces had already taken the necessary steps. We know that in Norway when the German troops went in, there were food supplies to last for a year. We know that Poland, though not a rich country, usually produces sufficient food for her people. Moreover, the other countries which Herr Hitler has invaded all held considerable stocks when the Germans entered and are themselves, in many cases, very substantial food producers. If all this food is not available now, it can only be because it has been removed to feed the people of Germany and to give them increased rations – for a change – during the last few months. At this season of the year and for some months to come, there is the least chance of scarcity as the harvest has just been gathered in. The only agencies which can create famine in any part of Europe, now and during the coming winter, will be German exactions or German failure to distribute the supplies which they command.

There is another aspect. Many of the most valuable foods are essential to the manufacture of vital war material. Fats are used to make explosives. Potatoes make the alcohol for motor spirit. The plastic materials now so largely used in the construction of aircraft are made of milk. If the Germans use these commodities to help them to bomb our women and children, rather than to feed the populations who produce them, we may be sure that imported foods would go the same way, directly or indirectly, or be employed to relieve the enemy of the responsibilities he has so wantonly assumed. Let Hitler bear his responsibilities to the full, and let the peoples of Europe who groan beneath his yoke aid in every way the coming of the day when that yoke will be broken. Meanwhile, we can and we will arrange in advance for the speedy entry of food into any part of the enslaved area, when this part has been wholly cleared of German forces, and has genuinely regained its freedom. We shall do our best to encourage the building up of reserves of food all over the world, so that there will always be held up before the eyes of the peoples of Europe, including – I say deliberately – the German and Austrian peoples, the certainty that the shattering of the Nazi power will bring to them all immediate food, freedom and peace.

Rather more than a quarter of a year has passed since the new Government came into power in this country. What a cataract of disaster has poured out upon us since then! The trustful Dutch overwhelmed; their beloved and respected Sovereign driven into exile; the peaceful city of Rotterdam the scene of a massacre as hideous and brutal as anything in the Thirty Years' War; Belgium invaded and beaten down; our own fine Expeditionary Force, which King Leopold called to his rescue, cut off and almost captured, escaping as it seemed only by a miracle and with the loss of all its equipment; our Ally, France, out; Italy in against us; all France in the power of the enemy, all its arsenals and vast masses of military material converted or convertible to the enemy's use; a puppet Government set up at Vichy which may at any moment be forced to become our foe; the whole western seaboard of Europe from the North Cape to the Spanish frontier in German hands; all the ports, all the airfields on this immense front employed against us as potential springboards of invasion. Moreover, the German air power, numerically so far outstripping ours, has been brought so close to our Island that what we used to dread greatly has come to pass and the hostile bombers not only reach our shores in a few minutes and from many directions, but can be escorted by their fighter aircraft. Why, Sir, if we had been confronted at the beginning of May with such a prospect, it would have seemed incredible that at the end of a period of horror and disaster, or at this point in a period of horror and disaster, we should stand erect, sure of ourselves, masters of our fate and with the conviction of final victory burning unquenchable in our hearts. Few would have believed we could survive; none would have believed that we should today not only feel stronger but should actually be stronger than we have ever been before.

Let us see what has happened on the other side of the scales. The British nation and the British Empire, finding themselves alone, stood undismayed against disaster. No one flinched or wavered; nay, some who formerly thought of peace, now think only of war. Our people are united and resolved, as they have never been before. Death and ruin have become small things compared with the shame of defeat or failure in duty. We cannot tell what lies ahead. It may be that even greater ordeals lie before us. We shall face whatever is coming to us. We are sure of ourselves and of our cause, and that is the supreme fact which has emerged in these months of trial.

Meanwhile, we have not only fortified our hearts but our Island. We have rearmed and rebuilt our armies in a degree which would have been deemed impossible a few months ago. We have ferried across the Atlantic, in the month of July, thanks to our friends over there, an immense mass of munitions of all kinds: cannon, rifles, machine guns, cartridges and shell, all safely landed without the loss of a gun or a round. The output of our own factories, working as they have never worked before, has poured forth to the troops. The whole British Army is at home. More than 2,000,000 determined men have rifles and bayonets in their hands tonight, and three-quarters of them are in regular military formations. We have never had armies like this in our Island in time of war. The whole Island bristles against invaders, from the sea or from the air. As I explained to the House in the middle of June, the stronger our Army at home, the larger must the invading expedition be, and the larger the invading expedition, the less difficult will be the task of the Navy in detecting its assembly and in intercepting and destroying it in passage; and the greater also would be the difficulty of feeding and supplying the invaders if ever they landed, in the teeth of continuous naval and air attack on their communications. All this is classical and venerable doctrine. As in Nelson's day, the maxim holds, 'Our first line of defence is the enemy's ports.' Now air reconnaissance and photography have brought to an old principle a new and potent aid.

Our Navy is far stronger than it was at the begining

of the war. The great flow of new construction set on foot at the outbreak is now beginning to come in. We hope our friends across the ocean will send us a timely reinforcement to bridge the gap between the peace flotillas of 1939 and the war flotillas of 1941. There is no difficulty in sending such aid. The seas and oceans are open. The U-boats are contained. The magnetic mine is, up to the present time, effectively mastered. The merchant tonnage under the British flag, after a year of unlimited U-boat war, after eight months of intensive mining attack, is larger than when we began. We have, in addition, under our control at least 4,000,000 tons of shipping from the captive countries which has taken refuge here or in the harbours of the Empire. Our stocks of food of all kinds are far more abundant than in the days of peace, and a large and growing programme of food production is on foot.

Why do I say all this? Not, assuredly, to boast; not, assuredly, to give the slightest countenance to complacency. The dangers we face are still enormous, but so are our advantages and resources. I recount them because the people have a right to know that there are solid grounds for the confidence which we feel, and that we have good reason to believe ourselves capable, as I said in a very dark hour two months ago, of continuing the war 'if necessary alone, if necessary for years'. I say it also because the fact that the British Empire stands invincible, and that Nazidom is still being resisted, will kindle again the spark of hope in the breasts of hundreds of millions of downtrodden or despairing men and women throughout Europe, and far beyond its bounds, and that from these sparks there will presently come cleansing and devouring flame.

The great air battle which has been in progress over this Island for the last few weeks has recently attained a high intensity. It is too soon to attempt to assign limits either to its scale or to its duration. We must certainly expect that greater efforts will be made by the enemy than any he has so far put forth. Hostile airfields are still being developed in France and the Low Countries, and the movement of squadrons and material for attacking us is still proceeding. It is quite plain that Herr Hitler could not admit defeat in his air attack on Great Britain without sustaining most serious injury. If after all his boastings and bloodcurdling threats and lurid accounts trumpeted round the world of the damage he has inflicted, of the vast numbers of our Air Force he has shot down, so he says, with so little loss to himself; if after tales of the panic-stricken British crushed in their holes cursing the plutocratic Parliament which has led them to such a plight – if after all this his whole air onslaught were forced after a while tamely to peter out, the Führer's reputation for veracity of statement might be seriously impugned. We may be sure, therefore, that he will continue as long as he has the strength to do so, and as long as any preoccupations he may have in respect of the Russian Air Force allow him to do so.

On the other hand, the conditions and course of the fighting have so far been favourable to us. I told the House two months ago that, whereas in France our fighter aircraft were wont to inflict a loss of two or three to one upon the Germans, and in the fighting at Dunkirk, which was a kind of no-man's-land, a loss of about three or four to one, we expected that in an attack on this Island we should achieve a larger ratio. This has certainly come true. It must also be remembered that all the enemy machines and pilots which are shot down over our Island, or over the seas which surround it, are either destroyed or captured; whereas a considerable proportion of our machines, and also of our pilots, are saved, and soon again in many cases come into action.

A vast and admirable system of salvage, directed by the Ministry of Aircraft Production, ensures the speediest return to the fighting line of damaged machines, and the most provident and speedy use of all the spare parts and material. At the same time the splendid – nay, astounding – increase in the output and repair of British aircraft and engines which Lord Beaverbrook has achieved by a genius of organization and drive, which looks like magic, has given us overflowing reserves of every type of aircraft, and an ever-mounting stream of production both in quantity and quality. The enemy is, of course, far more numerous than we are. But our new production already, as I am advised, largely exceeds his, and the American production is only just beginning to flow in. It is a fact, as I see from my daily returns, that our bomber and fighter strength now, after all this fighting, are larger than they have ever been. We believe that we shall be able to continue the air struggle indefinitely and as long as the enemy pleases, and the longer it continues the more rapid will be our approach, first towards that parity, and then into that superiority, in the air upon which in a large measure the decision of the war depends.

The gratitude of every home in our Island, in our Empire, and indeed throughout the world, except in the abodes of the guilty, goes out to the British airmen who, undaunted by odds, unwearied in their constant challenge and mortal danger, are turning the tide of the World War by their prowess and by their devotion. Never in the field of human conflict was so much owed by so many to so few. All hearts go out to the fighter pilots, whose brilliant actions we see with our own eyes day after day; but we must never forget that all the time, night after night, month after month, our bomber squadrons travel far into Germany, find their targets in the darkness by the highest navigational skill, aim their attacks, often under the heaviest fire, often with serious loss, with deliberate careful discrimination, and inflict shattering blows upon the whole of the technical and war-making structure of the Nazi power. On no part of the Royal Air Force does the weight of the war fall more heavily than on the daylight bombers, who will play an invaluable part in the case of invasion and whose unflinching zeal it has been necessary in the meanwhile on numerous occasions to restrain.

We are able to verify the results of bombing military targets in Germany, not only by reports which reach us through many sources, but also, of course, by photography. I have no hesitation in saying that this process of bombing the military industries and communications of Germany and the air bases and storage depots from which we are attacked, which process will continue upon an ever-increasing scale until the end of the war, and may in another year attain dimensions hitherto undreamed of, affords one at least of the most certain, if not the shortest, of all the roads to victory. Even if the Nazi legions stood triumphant on the Black Sea, or indeed upon the Caspian, even if Hitler was at the gates of India, it would profit him nothing if at the same time the entire economic and scientific apparatus of German war power lay shattered and pulverized at home.

The fact that the invasion of this Island upon a large scale has become a far more difficult operation with every week that has passed since we saved our Army at Dunkirk, and our very great preponderance of sea power enable us to turn our eyes and to turn our strength increasingly towards the Mediterranean and against that other enemy who, without the slightest provocation, coldly and deliberately, for greed and gain, stabbed France in the back in the moment of her agony, and is now marching against us in Africa. The defection of France has, of course, been deeply damaging to our position in what is called, somewhat oddly, the Middle East. In the defence of Somaliland, for instance, we had counted upon strong French forces attacking the Italians from Jibuti. We had counted also upon the use of the French naval and air bases in the Mediterranean, and particularly upon the North African shore. We had counted upon the French Fleet. Even though metropolitan France was temporarily overrun, there was no reason why the French Navy, substantial parts of the French Army, the French Air Force and the French Empire overseas should not have continued the struggle at our side.

Shielded by overwhelming sea power, possessed of invaluable strategic bases and of ample funds, France might have remained one of the great combatants in the struggle. By so doing, France would have preserved the continuity of her life, and the French Empire might have advanced with the British Empire to the rescue of the independence and integrity of the French Mother-land. In our own case, if we had been put in the terrible position of France, a contingency now happily impossible, although, of course, it would have been the duty of all war leaders to fight on here to the end, it would also have been their duty, as I indicated in my speech of 4th June, to provide as far as possible for the Naval security of Canada and our Dominions and to make sure they had the means to carry on the struggle from beyond the oceans. Most of the other countries that have been over-run by Germany for the time being have persevered valiantly and faithfully. The Czechs, the Poles, the Norwegians, the Dutch, the Belgians are still in the field, sword in hand, recognized by Great Britain and the United States as the sole representative authorities and lawful Governments of their respective States.

That France alone should lie prostrate at this moment is the crime, not of a great and noble nation, but of what are called 'the men of Vichy'. We have profound sympathy with the French people. Our old comradeship with France is not dead. In General de Gaulle and his gallant band, that comradeship takes an effective form. These free Frenchmen have been condemned to death by Vichy, but the day will come, as surely as the sun will rise tomorrow, when their names will be held in honour, and their names will be graven in stone in the streets and villages of a France restored in a liberated Europe to its full freedom and its ancient fame. But this conviction which I feel of the future cannot affect the immediate problems which confront us in the Mediterranean and in Africa. It had been decided some time before the beginning of the war not to defend the Protectorate of Somaliland. That policy was changed in the early months of the war. When the French gave in, and when our small forces there, a few battalions, a few guns, were attacked by all the Italian troops, nearly two divisions, which had formerly faced the French at Jibuti, it was right to withdraw our detachments, virtually intact, for action elsewhere. Far larger operations no doubt impend in the Middle East theatre, and I shall certainly not attempt to discuss or prophesy about their probable course. We have large armies and many means of reinforcing them. We have the complete sea command of the eastern Mediterranean. We intend to do our best to give a good account of ourselves, and to discharge faithfully and resolutely all our obligations and duties in that quarter of the world. More than that I do not think the House would wish me to say at the present time.

A good many people have written to me to ask me to make on this occasion a fuller statement of our war aims, and of the kind of peace we wish to make after the war, than is contained in the very considerable declaration which was made early in the autumn. Since then we have made common cause with Norway, Holland and Belgium. We have recognized the Czech Government of Dr Beneš, and we have told General de Gaulle that our success will carry with it the restoration of France. I do not think it would be wise at this moment, while the battle rages and the war is still perhaps only in its earlier stage, to embark upon elaborate speculations about the future shape which should be given to Europe or the new securities which must be arranged to spare mankind the miseries of a third World War. The ground is not new, it has been frequently traversed and explored, and many ideas are held about it in common by all good men, and all free men. But before we can undertake the task of rebuilding we have not only to be convinced ourselves, but we have to convince all other countries that the Nazi tyranny is going to be finally broken. The right to guide the course of world history is the noblest prize of victory. We are still toiling up the hill; we have not yet reached the crest-line of it; we cannot survey the landscape or even imagine what its condition will be when that longed-for morning comes. The task which lies before us immediately is at once more practical, more simple and more stern. I hope – indeed, I pray – that we shall not be found unworthy of our victory if after toil and tribulation it is granted to us. For the rest, we have to gain the victory. That is our task.

There is, however, one direction in which we can see a little more clearly ahead. We have to think not only for ourselves but for the lasting security of the cause and principle for which we are fighting and of the long future of the British Commonwealth of Nations. Some months ago we came to the conclusion that the interests of the United States and of the British Empire both required that the United States should have facilities for the naval and air defence of the Western Hemisphere against the attack of a Nazi power which might have acquired temporary but lengthy control of a large part of Western Europe and its formidable resources. We had therefore decided spontaneously, and without being asked or offered any inducement, to inform the Government of the United States that we would be glad to place such defence facilities at their disposal by leasing suitable sites in our Transatlantic possessions for their greater security against the unmeasured dangers of the future. The principle of association of interests for common purposes between Great Britain and the United States had developed even before the war. Various agreements had been reached about certain small islands in the Pacific Ocean which had become important as air fuelling points. In all this line of thought we found ourselves in very close harmony with the Government of Canada.

Presently we learned that anxiety was also felt in the United States about the air and naval defence of their Atlantic seaboard, and President Roosevelt has recently made it clear that he would like to discuss with us, and with the Dominion of Canada and with Newfoundland, the development of American naval and air facilities in Newfoundland and in the West Indies. There is, of course, no question of any transference of sovereignty – that has never been suggested – or of any action being taken without the consent or against the wishes of the various Colonies concerned; but for our part, His Majesty's Government are entirely willing to accord defence facilities to the United States on a 99 years' leasehold basis, and we feel sure that our interests no less than theirs, and the interests of the Colonies themselves and of Canada and Newfoundland, will be served thereby. These are important steps. Undoubtedly this process means that these two great organizations of the English-speaking democracies, the British Empire and the United States, will have to be somewhat mixed up together in some of their affairs for mutual and general advantage. For my own part, looking out upon the future, I do not view the process with any misgivings. I could not stop it if I wished; no one can stop it. Like the Mississippi, it just keeps rolling along. Let it roll. Let it roll on full flood, inexorable, irresistible, benignant, to broader lands and better days.

'We will all go down fighting to the end'

17 September 1940

Secret Session, House of Commons

Britain braces itself for invasion.

The reason why I asked the House to go into Secret Session was not because I had anything particularly secret or momentous to say. It was only because there are some things which it is better for us to talk over among ourselves than when we are overheard by the Germans. I wish to speak about the sittings of the House and how we are to discharge our Parliamentary duties . . .

We ought not to flatter ourselves by imagining that we are irreplaceable, but at the same time it cannot be denied that two or three hundred by-elections would be a quite needless complication of our affairs at this particular juncture. Moreover, I suppose that if Hitler made a clean sweep of the Houses of Parliament it would give widespread and unwholesome satisfaction throughout Germany, and be vaunted as another triumph for the Nazi system of government. We must exercise reasonable prudence and a certain amount of guile in combating the malice of the enemy. It is no part of good sense to proclaim the hour and dates of our meetings long beforehand . . .

These next few weeks are grave and anxious. I said just now in the Public Session that the deployment of the enemy's invasion preparations and the assembly of his ships and barges are steadily proceeding, and that any moment a major assault may be launched upon this island. I now say in secret that upwards of seventeen hundred self-propelled barges and more than two hundred seagoing ships, some very large ships, are already gathering at the many invasion ports in German occupation. If this is all a pretence and stratagem to pin us down here, it has been executed with surprising thoroughness and on a gigantic scale. Some of these ships and barges, when struck by our bombing counterattack and preventive attack, have blown up with tremendous explosions, showing that they are fully loaded with all the munitions needed for the invading armies and to beat us down and subjugate us utterly. The shipping available and now assembled is sufficient to carry in one voyage nearly *half a million* men. We should, of course, expect to drown a great many on the way over, and to destroy a large proportion of their vessels. But when you reflect upon the many points from which they could start, and upon the fact that even the most likely sector of invasion, i.e., the sector in which enemy fighter support is available for their bombers and dive bombers, extending from the Wash to the Isle of Wight, is nearly as long as the whole front in France from the Alps to the sea, and also upon the dangers of fog or artificial fog, one must expect many lodgments or attempted lodgments to be made on our island simultaneously. These we shall hope to deal with as they occur, and also to cut off the supply across the sea by which the enemy will seek to nourish his lodgments.

The difficulties of the invader are not ended when he sets foot on shore. A new chapter of perils opens upon him. I am confident that we shall succeed in defeating and largely destroying this most tremendous onslaught by which we are now threatened, and anyhow, whatever happens, we will all go down fighting to the end. I feel as sure as the sun will rise tomorrow that we shall be victorious.

'We can take it!'

8 October 1940

House of Commons

A month has passed since Herr Hitler turned his rage and malice on to the civil population of our great cities and particularly of London. He declared in his speech of 4th September that he would raze our cities to the ground, and since then he has been trying to carry out his fell purpose. Naturally, the first question we should ask is to what extent the full strength of the German bombing force has been deployed. I will give the House the best opinion I have been able to form on what is necessarily to some extent a matter of speculation. After their very severe mauling on 15 August, the German short-range dive bombers, of which there are several hundred, have been kept carefully out of the air fighting. This may be, of course, because they are being held in reserve so that they may play their part in a general plan of invasion or re-appear in some other theatre of war. We have, therefore, had to deal with the long-range German bombers alone.

It would seem that, taking day and night together, nearly 400 of these machines have, on the average, visited our shores every 24 hours. We are doubtful whether this rate of sustained attack could be greatly exceeded. . . .

Neither by material damage nor by slaughter will the people of the British Empire be turned from their solemn and inexorable purpose. It is the practice and in some cases the duty of many of my colleagues and many Members of the House to visit the scenes of destruction as promptly as possible, and I go myself from time to time. In all my life, I have never been treated with so much kindness as by the people who have suffered most. One would think one had brought some great benefit to them, instead of the blood and tears, the toil and sweat which is all I have ever promised. On every side, there is the cry, 'We can take it,' but with it, there is also the cry, 'Give it 'em back.' . . .

Meanwhile, what has happened to the invasion which we have been promised every month and almost every week since the beginning of July? Do not let us be lured into supposing that the danger is past. On the contrary, unwearying vigilance and the swift and steady strengthening of our Force by land, sea and air which is in progress must be at all costs maintained. Now that we are in October, however, the weather becomes very uncertain, and there are not many lucid intervals of two or three days together in which river barges can cross the narrow seas and land upon our beaches. Still, those intervals may occur. Fogs may aid the foe. Our Armies, which are growing continually in numbers, equipment, mobility and training, must be maintained all through the winter, not only along the beaches but in reserve, as the majority are, like leopards crouching to spring at the invader's throat. The enemy has certainly got prepared enough shipping and barges to throw half a million men in a single night on to salt water – or into it. The Home Guard, which now amounts to 1,700,000 men, must nurse their weapons and sharpen their bayonets. . . .

Because we feel easier in ourselves and see our way more clearly through our difficulties and dangers than we did some months ago, because foreign countries, friends or foes, recognize the giant, enduring, resilient strength of Britain and the British Empire, do not let us dull for one moment the sense of the awful hazards in which we stand. Do not let us lose the conviction that it is only by supreme and superb exertions, unwearying and indomitable, that we shall save our souls alive. No one can predict, no one can even imagine, how this terrible war against German and Nazi aggression will run its course or how far it will spread or how long it will last. Long, dark months of trials and tribulations lie before us. Not only great dangers, but many more misfortunes, many shortcomings, many mistakes, many disappointments will surely be our lot. Death and sorrow will be the companions of our journey; hardship our garment; constancy and valour our only shield. We must be united, we must be undaunted, we must be inflexible. Our qualities and deeds must burn and glow through the gloom of Europe until they become the veritable beacon of its salvation.

'Westward, look, the land is bright'

27 April 1941

Broadcast, London

Churchill's summary of the very difficult military situation faced by Britain.

I was asked last week whether I was aware of some uneasiness which it was said existed in the country on account of the gravity, as it was described, of the war situation. So I thought it would be a good thing to go and see for myself what this 'uneasiness' amounted to, and I went to some of our great cities and seaports which had been most heavily bombed, and to some of the places where the poorest people had got it worst. I have come back not only reassured, but refreshed. To leave the offices of Whitehall with their ceaseless hum of activity and stress, and to go out to the front, by which I mean the streets and wharves of London or Liverpool, Manchester, Cardiff, Swansea or Bristol, is like going out of a hothouse on to the bridge of a fighting ship. It is a tonic which I should recommend any who are suffering from fretfulness to take in strong doses when they have need of it.

It is quite true that I have seen many painful scenes of

havoc, and of fine buildings and acres of cottage homes blasted into rubble-heaps of ruin. But it is just in those very places where the malice of the savage enemy has done its worst, and where the ordeal of the men, women and children has been most severe, that I found their morale most high and splendid. Indeed, I felt encompassed by an exaltation of spirit in the people which seemed to lift mankind and its troubles above the level of material facts into that joyous serenity we think belongs to a better world than this.

Of their kindness to me I cannot speak, because I have never sought it or dreamed of it, and can never deserve it. I can only assure you that I and my colleagues, or comrades rather – for that is what they are – will toil with every scrap of life and strength, according to the lights that are granted to us, not to fail these people or be wholly unworthy of their faithful and generous regard. The British nation is stirred and moved as it has never been at any time in its long, eventful, famous history, and it is no hackneyed trope of speech to say that they mean to conquer or to die.

What a triumph the life of these battered cities is, over the worst that fire and bomb can do. What a vindication of the civilized and decent way of living we have been trying to work for and work towards in our Island. What a proof of the virtues of free institutions. What a test of the quality of our local authorities, and of institutions and customs and societies so steadily built. This ordeal by fire has even in a certain sense exhilarated the manhood and womanhood of Britain. The sublime but also terrible and sombre experiences and emotions of the battlefield which for centuries had been reserved for the soldiers and sailors, are now shared, for good or ill, by the entire population. All are proud to be under the fire of the enemy. Old men, little children, the crippled veterans of former wars, aged women, the ordinary hard-pressed citizen or subject of the King, as he likes to call himself, the sturdy workmen who swing the hammers or load the ships; skilful craftsmen; the members of every kind of ARP service, are proud to feel that they stand in the line together with our fighting men, when one of the greatest of causes is being fought out, as fought out it will be, to the end. This is indeed the grand heroic period of our history, and the light of glory shines on all.

You may imagine how deeply I feel my own responsibility to all these people; my responsibility to bear my part in bringing them safely out of this long, stern, scowling valley through which we are marching, and not to demand from them their sacrifices and exertions in vain.

I have thought in this difficult period, when so much fighting and so many critical and complicated manoeuvres are going on, that it is above all things important that our policy and conduct should be upon the highest level, and that honour should be our guide. Very few people realize how small were the forces with which General Wavell, that fine Commander whom we cheered in good days and will back through bad – how small were the forces which took the bulk of the Italian masses in Libya prisoners. In none of his successive victories could General Wavell maintain in the desert or bring into action more than two divisions, or about 30,000 men. When we reached Benghazi, and what was left of Mussolini's legions scurried back along the dusty road to Tripoli, a call was made upon us which we could not resist. Let me tell you about that call.

You will remember how in November the Italian Dictator fell upon the unoffending Greeks, and without reason and without warning invaded their country, and how the Greek nation, reviving their classic fame, hurled his armies back at the double-quick. Meanwhile Hitler, who had been creeping and worming his way steadily forward, doping and poisoning and pinioning, one after the other, Hungary, Rumania and Bulgaria, suddenly made it clear that he would come to the rescue of his fellow-criminal. The lack of unity among the Balkan States had enabled him to build up a mighty army in their midst. While nearly all the Greek troops were busy beating the Italians, the tremendous German military machine suddenly towered up on their other frontier. In their mortal peril the Greeks turned to us for succour. Strained as were our own resources, we could not say them nay. By solemn guarantee given before the war, Great Britain had promised them her help. They declared they would fight for their native soil even if neither of their neighbours made common cause with them, and even if we left them to their fate. But we could not do that. There are rules against that kind of thing; and to break those rules would be fatal to the honour of the British Empire, without which we could neither hope nor deserve to win this hard war. Military defeat or miscalculation can be redeemed. The fortunes of war are fickle and changing. But an act of shame would deprive us of the respect which we now enjoy throughout the world, and this would sap the vitals of our strength.

During the last year we have gained by our bearing and conduct a potent hold upon the sentiments of the people of the United States. Never, never in our history, have we been held in such admiration and regard across the Atlantic Ocean. In that great Republic, now in much travail and stress of soul, it is customary to use all the many valid, solid arguments about American interests and American safety, which depend upon the destruction of Hitler and his foul gang and even fouler doctrines. But in the long run – believe me, for I know – the action of the United States will be dictated, not by methodical calculations of profit and loss, but by moral sentiment, and by that gleaming flash of resolve which lifts the hearts of men and nations, and springs from the spiritual foundations of human life itself.

We, for our part, were of course bound to hearken to the Greek appeal to the utmost limit of our strength. We put the case to the Dominions of Australia and New Zealand, and their Governments, without in any way ignoring the hazards, told us that they felt the same as we did. So an important part of the mobile portion of the Army of the Nile was sent to Greece in fulfilment of our pledge. It happened that the divisions available and best suited to this task were from New Zealand and Australia, and that only about half the troops who took part in this dangerous expedition came from the Mother Country. I see the German propaganda is trying to make bad blood between us and Australia by making out that we have used them to do what we would not have asked of the

British Army. I shall leave it to Australia to deal with that taunt.

Let us see what has happened. We knew, of course, that the forces we could send to Greece would not by themselves alone be sufficient to stem the German tide of invasion. But there was a very real hope that the neighbours of Greece would by our intervention be drawn to stand in the line together with her while time remained. How nearly that came off will be known some day. The tragedy of Yugoslavia has been that these brave people had a government who hoped to purchase an ignoble immunity by submission to the Nazi will. Thus when at last the people of Yugoslavia found out where they were being taken, and rose in one spontaneous surge of revolt, they saved the soul and future of their country: but it was already too late to save its territory. They had no time to mobilize their armies. They were struck down by the ruthless and highly-mechanized Hun before they could even bring their armies into the field. Great disasters have occurred in the Balkans. Yugoslavia has been beaten down. Only in the mountains can she continue her resistance. The Greeks have been overwhelmed. Their victorious Albanian army has been cut off and forced to surrender, and it has been left to the Anzacs and their British comrades to fight their way back to the sea, leaving their mark on all who hindered them.

I turn aside from the stony path we have to tread, to indulge a moment of lighter relief. I daresay you have read in the newspapers that, by a special proclamation, the Italian Dictator has congratulated the Italian army in Albania on the glorious laurels they have gained by their victory over the Greeks. Here surely is the world's record in the domain of the ridiculous and the contemptible. This whipped jackal, Mussolini, who to save his own skin has made all Italy a vassal state of Hitler's Empire, comes frisking up at the side of the German tiger with yelpings not only of appetite – that can be understood – but even of triumph. Different things strike different people in different ways. But I am sure there are a great many millions in the British Empire and in the United States, who will find a new object in life in making sure that when we come to the final reckoning this absurd impostor will be abandoned to public justice and universal scorn.

While these grievous events were taking place in the Balkan Peninsula and in Greece, our forces in Libya have sustained a vexatious and damaging defeat. The Germans advanced sooner and in greater strength than we or our Generals expected. The bulk of our armoured troops, which had played such a decisive part in beating the Italians, had to be refitted, and the single armoured brigade which had been judged sufficient to hold the frontier till about the middle of May was worsted and its vehicles largely destroyed by a somewhat stronger German armoured force. Our Infantry, which had not exceeded one division, had to fall back upon the very large Imperial armies that have been assembled and can be nourished and maintained in the fertile delta of the Nile.

Tobruk – the fortress of Tobruk – which flanks any German advance on Egypt, we hold strongly. There we have repulsed many attacks, causing the enemy heavy losses and taking many prisoners. That is how the matter stands in Egypt and on the Libyan front.

We must now expect the war in the Mediterranean on the sea, in the desert, and above all in the air, to become very fierce, varied and widespread. We had cleaned the Italians out of Cyrenaica, and it now lies with us to purge that province of the Germans. That will be a harder task, and we cannot expect to do it at once. You know I never try to make out that defeats are victories. I have never underrated the German as a warrior. Indeed I told you a month ago that the swift, unbroken course of victories which we had gained over the Italians could not possibly continue, and that misfortunes must be expected. There is only one thing certain about war, that it is full of disappointments and also full of mistakes. It remains to be seen, however, whether it is the Germans who have made the mistake in trampling down the Balkan States and in making a river of blood and hate between themselves and the Greek and Yugoslav peoples. It remains also to be seen whether they have made a mistake in their attempt to invade Egypt with the forces and means of supply which they have now got. Taught by experience, I make it a rule not to prophesy about battles which have yet to be fought out. This, however, I will venture to say, that I should be very sorry to see the tasks of the combatants in the Middle East exchanged, and that General Wavell's armies should be in the position of the German invaders. That is only a personal opinion, and I can well understand you may take a different view. It is certain that fresh dangers besides those which threaten Egypt may come upon us in the Mediterranean. The war may spread to Spain and Morocco. It may spread eastward to Turkey and Russia. The Huns may lay their hands for a time upon the granaries of the Ukraine and the oil-wells of the Caucasus. They may dominate the Black Sea. They may dominate the Caspian. Who can tell? We shall do our best to meet them and fight them wherever they go. But there is one thing which is certain. There is one thing which rises out of the vast welter which is sure and solid, and which no one in his senses can mistake. Hitler cannot find safety from avenging justice in the East, in the Middle East, or in the Far East. In order to win this war, he must either conquer this Island by invasion, or he must cut the ocean lifeline which joins us to the United States.

Let us look into these alternatives, if you will bear with me for a few minutes longer. When I spoke to you last, early in February, many people believed the Nazi boastings that the invasion of Britain was about to begin. It has not begun yet, and with every week that passes we grow stronger on the sea, in the air, and in the numbers, quality, training and equipment of the great Armies that now guard our Island. When I compare the position at home as it is today with what it was in the summer of last year, even after making allowance for a much more elaborate mechanical preparation on the part of the enemy, I feel that we have very much to be thankful for, and I believe that, provided our exertions and our vigilance are not relaxed even for a moment, we may be confident that we shall give a very good account of ourselves. More than that it would be boastful to say. Less than that it would be foolish to believe.

But how about our lifeline across the Atlantic? What is to happen if so many of our merchant ships are sunk that we cannot bring in the food we need to nourish our brave people? What if the supplies of war materials and war weapons which the United States are seeking to send us in such enormous quantities should in large part be sunk on the way? What is to happen then? In February, as you may remember, that bad man in one of his raving outbursts threatened us with a terrifying increase in the numbers and activities of his U-boats and in his air attack – not only on our Island but, thanks to his use of French and Norwegian harbours, and thanks to the denial to us of the Irish bases – upon our shipping far out into the Atlantic. We have taken and are taking all possible measures to meet this deadly attack, and we are now fighting against it with might and main. That is what is called the Battle of the Atlantic, which in order to survive we have got to win on salt water just as decisively as we had to win the Battle of Britain last August and September in the air.

Wonderful exertions have been made by our Navy and Air Force; by the hundreds of mine-sweeping vessels which with their marvellous appliances keep our ports clear in spite of all the enemy can do; by the men who build and repair our immense fleets of merchant ships; by the men who load and unload them; and need I say by the officers and men of the Merchant Navy who go out in all weathers and in the teeth of all dangers to fight for the life of their native land and for a cause they comprehend and serve. Still, when you think how easy it is to sink ships at sea and how hard it is to build them and protect them, and when you remember that we have never less than two thousand ships afloat and three or four hundred in the danger zone; when you think of the great armies we are maintaining and reinforcing in the East, and of the world-wide traffic we have to carry on – when you remember all this, can you wonder that it is the Battle of the Atlantic which holds the first place in the thoughts of those upon whom rests the responsibility for procuring the victory?

It was therefore with indescribable relief that I learned of the tremendous decisions lately taken by the President and people of the United States. The American Fleet and flying boats have been ordered to patrol the wide waters of the Western Hemisphere, and to warn the peaceful shipping of all nations outside the combat zone of the presence of lurking U-boats or raiding cruisers belonging to the two aggressor nations. We British shall therefore be able to concentrate our protecting forces far more upon the routes nearer home, and to take a far heavier toll of the U-boats there. I have felt for some time that something like this was bound to happen. The President and Congress of the United States, having newly fortified themselves by contact with their electors, have solemnly pledged their aid to Britain in this war because they deem our cause just, and because they know their own interests and safety would be endangered if we were destroyed. They are taxing themselves heavily. They have passed great legislation. They have turned a large part of their gigantic industry to making the munitions which we need. They have even given us or lent us valuable weapons of their own. I could not believe that they would allow the high purposes to which they have set themselves to be frustrated and the products of their skill and

labour sunk to the bottom of the sea. U-boat warfare as
conducted by Germany is entirely contrary to international agreements freely subscribed to by Germany
only a few years ago. There is no effective blockade, but
only a merciless murder and marauding over wide, indis-
criminate areas utterly beyond the control of the German seapower. When I said ten weeks ago: 'Give us the
tools and we will finish the job,' I meant, *give* them to us:
put them within our reach – and that is what it now
seems the Americans are going to do. And that is why I
feel a very strong conviction that though the Battle of the
Atlantic will be long and hard, and its issue is by no means
yet determined, it has entered upon a more grim but at
the same time a far more favourable phase. When you
come to think of it, the United States are very closely
bound up with us now, and have engaged themselves
deeply in giving us moral, material and, within the limits
I have mentioned, naval support.

It is worthwhile therefore to take a look on both sides
of the ocean at the forces which are facing each other in
this awful struggle, from which there can be no drawing
back. No prudent and far-seeing man can doubt that the
eventual and total defeat of Hitler and Mussolini is certain, in view of the respective declared resolves of the
British and American democracies. There are less than
seventy million malignant Huns – some of whom are
curable and others killable – many of whom are already
engaged in holding down Austrians, Czechs, Poles, French,
and the many other ancient races they now bully and
pillage. The peoples of the British Empire and of the
United States number nearly two hundred millions in

their homelands and in the British Dominions alone. They possess the unchallengeable command of the oceans, and will soon obtain decisive superiority in the air. They have more wealth, more technical resources, and they make more steel, than the whole of the rest of the world put together. They are determined that the cause of freedom shall not be trampled down, nor the tide of world progress turned backwards, by the criminal Dictators.

While therefore we naturally view with sorrow and anxiety much that is happening in Europe and in Africa, and may happen in Asia, we must not lose our sense of proportion and thus become discouraged or alarmed. When we face with a steady eye the difficulties which lie before us, we may derive new confidence from remembering those we have already overcome. Nothing that is happening now is comparable in gravity with the dangers through which we passed last year. Nothing that can happen in the East is comparable with what is happening in the West.

Last time I spoke to you I quoted the lines of Longfellow which President Roosevelt had written out for me in his own hand. I have some other lines which are less well known but which seem apt and appropriate to our fortunes tonight, and I believe they will be so judged wherever the English language is spoken or the flag of freedom flies:

> For while the tired waves, vainly breaking,
> Seem here no painful inch to gain,

'Westward, look, the land is bright'

Far back, through creeks and inlets making,
Comes silent, flooding in, the main.
And not by eastern windows only,
When daylight comes, comes in the light;
In front the sun climbs slow, how slowly!
But westward, look, the land is bright.

Alliance with Russia

22 June 1941

Broadcast, London

Churchill addresses the nation following news that Hitler has invaded the USSR.

I have taken occasion to speak to you tonight because we have reached one of the climacterics of the war. The first of these intense turning-points was a year ago when France fell prostrate under the German hammer, and when we had to face the storm alone. The second was when the Royal Air Force beat the Hun raiders out of the daylight air, and thus warded off the Nazi invasion of our island while we were still ill-armed and ill-prepared. The third turning-point was when the President and Congress of the United States passed the Lease-and-Lend enactment, devoting nearly 2,000 millions sterling of wealth of the New World to help us to defend our liberties and their own. Those were the three climacterics. The fourth is now upon us.

At four o'clock this morning Hitler attacked and invaded Russia. All his usual formalities of perfidy were observed with scrupulous technique. A non-aggression treaty had been solemnly signed and was in force between the two countries. No complaint had been made by Germany of its non-fulfilment. Under its cloak of false confidence, the German armies drew up in immense strength along a line which stretches from the White Sea to the Black Sea; and their air fleets and armoured divisions slowly and methodically took their stations. Then, suddenly, without declaration of war, without even an ultimatum, German bombs rained down from the air upon the Russian cities, the German troops violated the frontiers; and an hour later the German Ambassador, who till the night before was lavishing his assurances of friendship, almost of alliance, upon the Russians, called upon the Russian Foreign Minister to tell him that a state of war existed between Germany and Russia.

Thus was repeated on a far larger scale the same kind of outrage against every form of signed compact and international faith which we have witnessed in Norway, Denmark, Holland and Belgium, and which Hitler's accomplice, the jackal Mussolini, so faithfully imitated in the case of Greece.

All this was no surprise to me. In fact I gave clear and precise warnings to Stalin of what was coming. I gave him warning as I have given warning to others before. I can only hope that this warning did not fall unheeded. All we know at present is that the Russian people are defending their native soil and that their leaders have called upon them to resist to the utmost.

Hitler is a monster of wickedness, insatiable in his lust for blood and plunder. Not content with having all Europe under his heel, or else terrorized into various forms of abject submission, he must now carry his work of butchery and desolation among the vast multitudes of Russia and of Asia. The terrible military machine, which we and the rest of the civilized world so foolishly, so supinely, so insensately allowed the Nazi gangsters to build up year by year from almost nothing, cannot stand idle lest it rust or fall to pieces. It must be in continual motion, grinding up human lives and trampling down the homes and the rights of hundreds of millions of men. Moreover it must be fed, not only with flesh but with oil.

So now this bloodthirsty guttersnipe must launch his mechanized armies upon new fields of slaughter, pillage and devastation. Poor as are the Russian peasants, workmen and soldiers, he must steal from them their daily bread; he must devour their harvests; he must rob them of the oil which drives their ploughs; and thus produce a famine without example in human history. And even the carnage and ruin which his victory, should he gain it – he has not gained it yet – will bring upon the Russian people, will itself be only a stepping-stone to the attempt to plunge the four or five hundred millions who live in China, and the three hundred and fifty millions who live in India, into that bottomless pit of human degradation over which the diabolic emblem of the Swastika flaunts itself. It is not too much to say here this summer evening that the lives and happiness of a thousand million additional people are now menaced with brutal Nazi violence. That is enough to make us hold our breath. But presently I shall show you something else that lies behind, and something that touches very nearly the life of Britain and of the United States.

The Nazi régime is indistinguishable from the worst features of Communism. It is devoid of all theme and principle except appetite and racial domination. It excels all forms of human wickedness in the efficiency of its cruelty and ferocious aggression. No one has been a more consistent opponent of Communism than I have for the last twenty-five years. I will unsay no word that I have spoken about it. But all this fades away before the spectacle which is now unfolding. The past with its crimes, its follies and its tragedies, flashes away. I see the Russian soldiers standing on the threshold of their native land, guarding the fields which their fathers have tilled from time immemorial. I see them guarding their homes where mothers and wives pray – ah yes, for there are times when all pray – for the safety of their loved ones, the return of the breadwinner, of their champion, of their protector. I see the ten thousand villages of Russia, where the means of existence was wrung so hardly from the soil, but where there are still primordial human joys, where maidens laugh and children play. I see advancing upon all this in hideous onslaught the Nazi war machine, with its clanking, heel-clicking, dandified Prussian officers, its crafty expert agents fresh from the cowing and tying-down of a dozen countries. I see also the dull, drilled, docile, brutish masses of the Hun soldiery plodding on like a swarm of crawling locusts. I see the German bombers and fighters in the sky, still smarting from many a British whipping, delighted to find what they believe is an easier and a safer prey.

Behind all this glare, behind all this storm, I see that small group of villainous men who plan, organise and launch this cataract of horrors upon mankind. And then my mind goes back across the years to the days when the Russian armies were our allies against the same deadly foe; when they fought with so much valour and constancy, and helped to gain a victory from all share in which, alas, they were – through no fault of ours – utterly cut off. I have lived through all this, and you will pardon me if I express my feelings and the stir of old memories.

But now I have to declare the decision of His Majesty's Government – and I feel sure it is a decision in which the great Dominions will, in due course, concur – for we must speak out now at once, without a day's delay. I have to make the declaration, but can you doubt what our policy will be? We have but one aim and one single, irrevocable purpose. We are resolved to destroy Hitler and every vestige of the Nazi régime. From this nothing will turn us – nothing. We will never parley, we will never negotiate with Hitler or any of his gang. We shall fight him by land, we shall fight him by sea, we shall fight him in the air, until with God's help we have rid the earth of his shadow and liberated its peoples from his yoke. Any man or state who fights on against Nazidom will have our aid. Any man or state who marches with Hitler is our foe. This applies not only to organized states but to all representatives of that vile race of quislings who make themselves the tools and agents of the Nazi régime against their fellow-countrymen and the lands of their birth. They – these quislings – like the Nazi leaders themselves, if not disposed of by their fellow-countrymen, which would save trouble, will be delivered by us on the morrow of victory to the justice of the Allied tribunals. That is our policy and that is our declaration. It follows, therefore, that we shall give whatever help we can to Russia and the Russian people. We shall appeal to all our friends and allies in every part of the world to take the same course and pursue it, as we shall, faithfully and steadfastly to the end.

We have offered the Government of Soviet Russia any technical or economic assistance which is in our power, and which is likely to be of service to them. We shall bomb Germany by day as well as by night in ever-increasing measure, casting upon them month by month a heavier discharge of bombs, and making the German people taste and gulp each month a sharper dose of the miseries they have showered upon mankind. It is noteworthy that only yesterday the Royal Air Force, fighting inland over French territory, cut down with very small loss to themselves 28 of the Hun fighting machines in the air above the French soil they have invaded, defiled and profess to hold. But this is only a beginning. From now forward the main expansion of our Air Force proceeds with gathering speed. In another six months the weight of the help we are receiving from the United States in war materials of all kinds, and especially in heavy bombers, will begin to tell.

This is no class war, but a war in which the whole British Empire and Commonwealth of Nations is engaged without distinction of race, creed or party. It is not for me to speak of the action of the United States, but this I will say: if Hitler imagines that his attack on Soviet Russia will cause the slightest division of aims or slackening of effort in the great Democracies who are resolved upon his doom, he is woefully mistaken. On the contrary, we shall be fortified and encouraged in our efforts to rescue mankind from his tyranny. We shall be strengthened and not weakened in determination and in resources.

This is no time to moralize on the follies of countries and governments which have allowed themselves to be struck down one by one, when by united action they could have saved themselves and saved the world from this catastrophe. But when I spoke a few minutes ago of Hitler's blood-lust and the hateful appetites which have impelled or lured him on his Russian adventure, I said there was one deeper motive behind his outrage. He wishes to destroy the Russian power because he hopes that if he succeeds in this, he will be able to bring back the main strength of his army and air force from the East and hurl it upon this Island, which he knows he must conquer or suffer the penalty of his crimes. His invasion of Russia is no more than a prelude to an attempted invasion of the British Isles. He hopes, no doubt, that all this may be accomplished before the winter comes, and that he can overwhelm Great Britain before the fleet and air power of the United States may intervene. He hopes that he may once again repeat, upon a greater scale than ever before, that process of destroying his enemies one by one, by which he has so long thrived and prospered, and that then the scene will be clear for the final act, without which all his conquests would be in vain – namely, the subjugation of the Western Hemisphere to his will and to his system.

The Russian danger is therefore our danger, and the

danger of the United States, just as the cause of any Russian fighting for his hearth and home is the cause of free men and free peoples in every quarter of the globe. Let us learn the lessons already taught by such cruel experience. Let us redouble our exertions, and strike with united strength while life and power remain.

The Atlantic Charter

24 August 1941

Broadcast, London

Churchill had just returned from Newfoundland, where he had met with President Roosevelt.

I thought you would like me to tell you something about the voyage which I made across the ocean to meet our great friend, the President of the United States. Exactly where we met is a secret, but I don't think I shall be indiscreet if I go so far as to say that it was 'somewhere in the Atlantic'.

In a spacious, landlocked bay which reminded me of the West Coast of Scotland, powerful American warships protected by strong flotillas and far-ranging aircraft awaited our arrival, and, as it were, stretched out a hand to help us in. Our party arrived in the newest, or almost the newest, British battleship, the *Prince of Wales*, with a modern escort of British and Canadian destroyers, and there for three days I spent my time in company, and I think I may say in comradeship, with Mr Roosevelt; while all the time the chiefs of the staff and the naval and military commanders both of the British Empire and of the United States sat together in continual council.

President Roosevelt is the thrice-chosen head of the

most powerful state and community in the world. I am the servant of King and Parliament at present charged with the principal direction of our affairs in these fateful times, and it is my duty also to make sure, as I have made sure, that anything I say or do in the exercise of my office is approved and sustained by the whole British Commonwealth of Nations. Therefore this meeting was bound to be important, because of the enormous forces at present only partially mobilized but steadily mobilizing which are at the disposal of these two major groupings of the human family: the British Empire and the United States, who, fortunately for the progress of mankind, happen to speak the same language, and very largely think the same thoughts, or anyhow think a lot of the same thoughts.

The meeting was therefore symbolic. That is its prime importance. It symbolizes, in a form and manner which everyone can understand in every land and in every clime, the deep underlying unities which stir and at decisive moments rule the English-speaking peoples throughout the world. Would it be presumptuous for me to say that it symbolizes something even more majestic – namely, the marshalling of the good forces of the world against the evil forces which are now so formidable and triumphant and which have cast their cruel spell over the whole of Europe and a large part of Asia?

This was a meeting which marks for ever in the pages of history the taking-up by the English-speaking nations, amid all this peril, tumult and confusion, of the guidance of the fortunes of the broad toiling masses in all the continents; and our loyal effort without any clog of selfish interest to lead them forward out of the miseries into which they have been plunged back to the broad high-road of freedom and justice. This is the highest honour and the most glorious opportunity which could ever have come to any branch of the human race.

When one beholds how many currents of extraordinary and terrible events have flowed together to make this harmony, even the most sceptical person must have the feeling that we all have the chance to play our part and do our duty in some great design, the end of which no mortal can foresee. Awful and horrible things are happening in these days. The whole of Europe has been wrecked and trampled down by the mechanical weapons and barbaric fury of the Nazis; the most deadly instruments of war-science have been joined to the extreme refinements of treachery and the most brutal exhibitions of ruthlessness, and thus have formed a combine of aggression the like of which has never been known, before which the rights, the traditions, the characteristics and the structure of many ancient honoured states and peoples have been laid prostrate and are now ground down under the heel and terror of a monster. The Austrians, the Czechs, the Poles, the Norwegians, the Danes, the Belgians, the Dutch, the Greeks, the Croats and the Serbs, above all the great French nation, have been stunned and pinioned. Italy, Hungary, Rumania, Bulgaria have bought a shameful respite by becoming the jackals of the tiger, but their situation is very little different and will presently be indistinguishable from that of his victims. Sweden, Spain and Turkey stand appalled, wondering which will be struck down next.

Here, then, is the vast pit into which all the most

famous states and races of Europe have been flung and from which unaided they can never climb. But all this did not satiate Adolf Hitler; he made a treaty of non-aggression with Soviet Russia, just as he made one with Turkey, in order to keep them quiet till he was ready to attack them, and then, nine weeks ago today, without a vestige of provocation, he hurled millions of soldiers, with all their apparatus, upon the neighbour he had called his friend, with the avowed object of destroying Russia and tearing her in pieces. This frightful business is now unfolding day by day before our eyes. Here is a devil who, in a mere spasm of his pride and lust for domination, can condemn two or three millions, perhaps it may be many more, of human beings, to speedy and violent death. 'Let Russia be blotted out – Let Russia be destroyed. Order the armies to advance.' Such were his decrees. Accordingly from the Arctic Ocean to the Black Sea, six or seven millions of soldiers are locked in mortal struggle. Ah, but this time it was not so easy.

This time it was not all one way. The Russian armies and all the peoples of the Russian Republic have rallied to the defence of their hearths and homes. For the first time Nazi blood has flowed in a fearful torrent. Certainly 1,500,000, perhaps 2,000,000 of Nazi cannon-fodder have bit the dust of the endless plains of Russia. The tremendous battle rages along nearly 2,000 miles of front. The Russians fight with magnificent devotion; not only that, our generals who have visited the Russian front line report with admiration the efficiency of their military organization and the excellence of their equipment. The aggressor is surprised, startled, staggered. For the first time in his experience mass murder has become unprofitable. He retaliates by the most frightful cruelties. As his armies advance, whole districts are being exterminated. Scores of thousands – literally scores of thousands – of executions in cold blood are being perpetrated by the German police-troops upon the Russian patriots who defend their native soil. Since the Mongol invasions of Europe in the sixteenth century, there has never been methodical, merciless butchery on such a scale, or approaching such a scale. And this is but the beginning. Famine and pestilence have yet to follow in the bloody ruts of Hitler's tanks. We are in the presence of a crime without a name.

But Europe is not the only continent to be tormented and devastated by aggressions. For five long years the Japanese military factions, seeking to emulate the style of Hitler and Mussolini, taking all their posturing as if it were a new European revelation, have been invading and harrying the 500,000,000 inhabitants of China. Japanese armies have been wandering about that vast land in futile excursions, carrying with them carnage, ruin and corruption and calling it the 'Chinese Incident'. Now they stretch a grasping hand into the southern seas of China; they snatch Indo-China from the wretched Vichy French; they menace by their movements Siam; menace Singapore, the British link with Australia; and menace the Philippine Islands under the protection of the United States. It is certain that this has got to stop. Every effort will be made to secure a peaceful settlement. The United States are labouring with infinite patience to arrive at a fair and amicable settlement which will give Japan the utmost reassurance for her legitimate interests. We earnestly hope these negotiations will succeed. But this I must say: that if these hopes should fail we shall of course range ourselves unhesitatingly at the side of the United States.

And thus we come back to the quiet bay somewhere in the Atlantic where misty sunshine plays on great ships which carry the White Ensign, or the Stars and Stripes. We had the idea, when we met there – the President and I – that without attempting to draw up final and formal peace aims, or war aims, it was necessary to give all peoples, especially the oppressed and conquered peoples, a simple, rough-and-ready wartime statement of the goal towards which the British Commonwealth and the United States mean to make their way, and thus make a way for others to march with them upon a road which will certainly be painful, and may be long!

There are, however, two distinct and marked differences in this joint declaration from the attitude adopted by the Allies during the latter part of the last war; and no one should overlook them. The United States and Great Britain do not now assume that there will never be any more war again. On the contrary, we intend to take ample precautions to prevent its renewal in any period we can foresee by effectively disarming the guilty nations while remaining suitably protected ourselves.

The second difference is this: that instead of trying to ruin German trade by all kinds of additional trade barriers and hindrances as was the mood of 1917, we have definitely adopted the view that it is not in the interests of the world and of our two countries that any large nation should be unprosperous or shut out from the means of making a decent living for itself and its people by its industry and enterprise. These are far-reaching changes of principle upon which all countries should ponder. Above all, it was necessary to give hope and the assurance of final victory to those many scores of millions of men and women who are battling for life and freedom, or who are already bent down under the Nazi yoke. Hitler and his confederates have for some time past been adjuring, bullying and beseeching the populations whom they have wronged and injured, to bow to their fate, to resign themselves to their servitude, and for the sake of some mitigations and indulgences, to 'collaborate' – that is the word – in what is called the New Order in Europe.

What is this New Order which they seek to fasten first upon Europe and if possible – for their ambitions are boundless – upon all the continents of the globe? It is the rule of the *Herrenvolk* – the master-race – who are to put an end to democracy, to parliaments, to the fundamental freedoms and decencies of ordinary men and women, to the historic rights of nations; and give them in exchange the iron rule of Prussia, the universal goose-step, and a strict, efficient discipline enforced upon the working class by the political police, with the German concentration camps and firing parties, now so busy in a dozen lands, always handy in the background. There is the New Order.

Napoleon in his glory and his genius spread his Empire far and wide. There was a time when only the snows of Russia and the white cliffs of Dover with their guardian fleets stood between him and the dominion of the world. Napoleon's armies had a theme: they carried with them the surges of the French Revolution. Liberty, Equality and Fraternity – that was the cry. There was a sweeping away of outworn medieval systems and aristocratic privilege. There was the land for the people, a new code of law. Nevertheless, Napoleon's Empire vanished like a dream. But Hitler, Hitler has no theme, naught but mania, appetite and exploitation. He has, however, weapons and machinery for grinding down and for holding down conquered countries which are the product, the sadly perverted product, of modern science.

The ordeals, therefore, of the conquered peoples will be hard. We must give them hope; we must give them the conviction that their sufferings and their resistances will not be in vain. The tunnel may be dark and long, but at the end there is light. That is the symbolism and that is the message of the Atlantic meeting. Do not despair, brave Norwegians: your land shall be cleansed not only from the invader but from the filthy quislings who are his tools. Be sure of yourselves, Czechs: your independence shall be restored. Poles, the heroism of your people standing up to cruel oppressors, the courage of your soldiers, sailors and airmen, shall not be forgotten: your country shall live again and resume its rightful part in the new organization of Europe. Lift up your heads, gallant Frenchmen: not all the infamies of Darlan and of Laval shall stand between you and the restoration of your birthright. Tough, stout-hearted Dutch, Belgians, Luxembourgers, tormented, mishandled, shamefully castaway peoples of Yugoslavia, glorious Greece, now subjected to the crowning insult of the rule of the Italian jackanapes; yield not an inch! Keep your souls clean from all contact with the Nazis; make them feel even in their fleeting hour of brutish triumph that they are the moral outcasts of mankind. Help is coming; mighty forces are arming on your behalf. Have faith. Have hope. Deliverance is sure.

There is the signal which we have flashed across the water; and if it reaches the hearts of those to whom it is sent, they will endure with fortitude and tenacity their present misfortunes in the sure faith that they, too, are still serving the common cause, and that their efforts will not be in vain.

You will perhaps have noticed that the President of the United States and the British representative, in what is aptly called the 'Atlantic Charter', have jointly pledged their countries to the final destruction of the Nazi tyranny. That is a solemn and grave undertaking. It must be made good; it will be made good. And, of course, many practical arrangements to fulfil that purpose have been and are being organized and set in motion.

The question has been asked: how near is the United States to war? There is certainly one man who knows the answer to that question. If Hitler has not yet declared war upon the United States, it is surely not out of his love for American institutions; it is certainly not because he could not find a pretext. He has murdered half a dozen countries for far less. Fear of immediately redoubling the tremendous energies now being employed against him is no doubt a restraining influence. But the real reason is, I am sure, to be found in the method to which he has so faithfully adhered and by which he has gained so much.

What is that method? It is a very simple method. One by one: that is his plan; that is his guiding rule; that is the trick by which he has enslaved so large a portion of the world. Three and a half years ago I appealed to my fellow-countrymen to take the lead in weaving together a strong defensive union within the principles of the League of Nations, a union of all the countries who felt themselves in evergrowing danger. But none would listen; all stood idle while Germany rearmed. Czechoslovakia was subjugated; a French Government deserted their faithful ally and broke a plighted word in that ally's hour of need. Russia was cajoled and deceived into a kind of neutrality or partnership, while the French Army was being annihilated. The Low Countries and the Scandinavian countries, acting with France and Great Britain in good time, even after the war had begun, might have altered its course, and would have had, at any rate, a fighting chance. The Balkan States had only to stand together to save themselves from the ruin by which they are now engulfed. But one by one they were undermined and overwhelmed. Never was the career of crime made more smooth.

Now Hitler is striking at Russia with all his might, well knowing the difficulties of geography which stand between Russia and the aid which the Western Democracies are trying to bring. We shall strive our utmost to overcome all obstacles and to bring this aid. We have arranged for a conference in Moscow between the United States, British and Russian authorities to settle the whole plan. No barrier must stand in the way. But why is Hitler striking at Russia, and inflicting and suffering himself or, rather, making his soldiers suffer, this frightful slaughter? It is with the declared object of turning his whole force upon the British Islands, and if he could succeed in beating the life and the strength out of us, which is not so easy, then is the moment when he will settle his account, and it is already a long one, with the people of the United States and generally with the Western Hemisphere. One by one, there is the process; there is the simple, dismal plan which has served Hitler so well. It needs but one final successful application to make him the master of the world. I am devoutly thankful that some eyes at least are fully opened to it while time remains. I rejoiced to find that the President saw in their true light and proportion the extreme dangers by which the American people as well as the British people are now beset. It was indeed by the mercy of God that he began eight years ago that revival of the strength of the American Navy without which the New World today would have to take its orders from the European dictators, but with which the United States still retains the power to marshal her gigantic strength, and in saving herself to render an incomparable service to mankind.

We had a church parade on the Sunday in our Atlantic bay. The President came on to the quarter-deck of the *Prince of Wales*, where there were mingled together many hundreds of American and British sailors and marines. The sun shone bright and warm while we all sang the old hymns which are our common inheritance and which we learned as children in our homes. We sang the hymn founded on the psalms which John Hampden's soldiers sang when they bore his body to the grave, and in which the brief, precarious span of human life is contrasted with the immutability of Him to Whom a thousand ages are but as yesterday, and as a watch in the night. We sang the sailors' hymn 'For those in peril' – and there are very many – 'on the sea'. We sang 'Onward Christian Soldiers'. And indeed I felt that this was no vain presumption, but that we had the right to feel that we were serving a cause for the sake of which a trumpet has sounded from on high.

When I looked upon that densely packed congregation of fighting men of the same language, of the same faith, of the same fundamental laws and the same ideals, and now to a large extent of the same interests, and certainly in different degrees facing the same dangers, it swept across me that here was the only hope, but also the sure hope, of saving the world from measureless degradation.

And so we came back across the ocean waves, uplifted in spirit, fortified in resolve. Some American destroyers which were carrying mails to the United States marines in Iceland happened to be going the same way, too, so we made a goodly company at sea together.

And when we were right out in mid-passage one afternoon a noble sight broke on the view. We overtook one of the convoys which carry the munitions and supplies of the New World to sustain the champions of freedom in the Old. The whole broad horizon seemed filled with ships; seventy or eighty ships of all kinds and sizes, arrayed in fourteen lines, each of which could have been drawn with a ruler, hardly a wisp of smoke, not a straggler, but all bristling with cannons and other precautions on which I will not dwell, and all surrounded by their British escorting vessels, while overhead the far-ranging Catalina air-boats soared – vigilant, protecting eagles in the sky. Then I felt that – hard and terrible and long drawn-out as this struggle may be – we shall not be denied the strength to do our duty to the end.

'The bright gleam of victory'

10 November 1942

*The Lord Mayor's Luncheon,
Mansion House, London*

Churchill's response to the Second Battle of El Alamein.

I have never promised anything but blood, tears, toil, and sweat. Now, however, we have a new experience. We have victory – a remarkable and definite victory. The bright gleam has caught the helmets of our soldiers, and warmed and cheered all our hearts.

The late M. Venizelos observed that in all her wars England – he should have said Britain, of course – always wins one battle – the last. It would seem to have begun rather earlier this time. General Alexander, with his brilliant comrade and lieutenant, General Montgomery, has gained a glorious and decisive victory in what I think should be called the Battle of Egypt. Rommel's army has been defeated. It has been routed. It has been very largely destroyed as a fighting force.

This battle was not fought for the sake of gaining positions or so many square miles of desert territory. General Alexander and General Montgomery fought it with one single idea. They meant to destroy the armed force of the enemy, and to destroy it at the place where the disaster would be most far-reaching and irrecoverable.

All the various elements in our line of battle played their parts – Indian troops, Fighting French, the Greeks, the representatives of Czechoslovakia and the others who took part. The Americans rendered powerful and invaluable service in the air. But as it happened – as the course of the battle turned – it has been fought throughout almost entirely by men of British blood from home and from the Dominions on the one hand, and by Germans on the other. The Italians were left to perish in the waterless desert or surrender as they are doing.

The fight between the British and the Germans was intense and fierce in the extreme. It was a deadly grapple. The Germans have been outmatched and outfought with the very kind of weapons with which they had beaten down so many small peoples, and also large unprepared peoples. They have been beaten by the very technical apparatus on which they counted to gain them the domination of the world. Especially is this true of the air and of the tanks and of the artillery, which has come back into its own on the battlefield. The Germans have received back again that measure of fire and steel which they have so often meted out to others.

Now this is not the end. It is not even the begining of the end. But it is, perhaps, the end of the beginning. Henceforth Hitler's Nazis will meet equally well armed, and perhaps better-armed troops. Henceforth they will have to face in many theatres of war that superiority in the air which they have so often used without mercy against others, of which they boasted all round the world, and which they intended to use as an instrument for convincing all other peoples that all resistance to them was hopeless. When I read of the coastal road crammed with fleeing German vehicles under the blasting attacks of the Royal Air Force, I could not but remember those roads of France and Flanders, crowded, not with fighting men, but with helpless refugees – women and children – fleeing with their pitiful barrows and household goods, upon whom such merciless havoc was wreaked. I have, I trust, a humane disposition, but I must say I could not help feeling that what was happening, however grievous, was only justice grimly reclaiming her rights.

It will be my duty in the near future to give to Parliament a full and particular account of these operations. All I will say of them at present is that the victory which has already been gained gives good prospect of becoming decisive and final so far as the defence of Egypt is concerned.

But this Battle of Egypt, in itself so important, was designed and timed as a prelude and counterpart of the momentous enterprise undertaken by the United States at the western end of the Mediterranean – an enterprise under United States command in which our Army, Air Force, and, above all, our Navy, are bearing an honourable and important share. Very full accounts have been published of all that is happening in Morocco, Algeria and Tunis. The President of the United States, who is Commander-in-Chief of the armed forces of America, is the author of this mighty undertaking, and in all of it I have been his active and ardent lieutenant. . . .

At this time our thoughts turn towards France, groaning

in bondage under the German heel. Many ask themselves the question: Is France finished? Is that long and
famous history, adorned by so many manifestations of
genius and valour, bearing with it so much that is pre-
cious to culture and civilization, and above all to the liberties of mankind – is all that now to sink for ever into the
ocean of the past, or will France rise again and resume
her rightful place in the structure of what may one day
be again the family of Europe? I declare to you here, on
this considerable occasion, even now when misguided or
suborned Frenchmen are firing upon their rescuers, I
declare to you my faith that France will rise again. While
there are men like General de Gaulle and all those who
follow him – and they are legion throughout France –
and men like General Giraud, that gallant warrior whom
no prison can hold, while there are men like those to
stand forward in the name and in the cause of France, my
confidence in the future of France is sure.

For ourselves we have no wish but to see France free
and strong, with her Empire gathered round her and
with Alsace-Lorraine restored. We covet no French possession; we have no acquisitive appetites or ambitions in
North Africa or any other part of the world. We have not
entered this war for profit or expansion, but only for honour and to do our duty in defending the right.

Let me, however, make this clear, in case there should
be any mistake about it in any quarter. We mean to hold
our own. I have not become the King's First Minister in
order to preside over the liquidation of the British Empire.
For that task, if ever it were prescribed, someone else
would have to be found, and, under democracy, I suppose

the nation would have to be consulted. I am proud to be a member of that vast commonwealth and society of nations and communities gathered in and around the ancient British monarchy, without which the good cause might well have perished from the face of the earth. Here we are, and here we stand, a veritable rock of salvation in this drifting world.

'The Desert Army'

3 February 1943

Tripoli

Churchill's address to some 2,000 men of the Eighth Army.

The last time I saw this army was in the closing days of August on those sandy and rocky bluffs near Alamein and the Ruweisat ridge, when it was apparent from all the signs that Rommel was about to make his final thrust on Alexandria and Cairo. Then all was to be won or lost. Now I come to you a long way from Alamein, and I find this army and its famous commander with a record of victory behind it which has undoubtedly played a decisive part in altering the whole character of the war.

The fierce and well-fought battle of Alamein, the blasting through of the enemy's seaward flank, and the thunderbolt of the armoured attack, irretrievably broke the army which Rommel had boasted would conquer Egypt, and upon which the German and Italian peoples had set their hopes. Thereafter and ever since, in these remorseless three months, you have chased this hostile army and driven it from pillar to post over a distance of more than 1,400 miles – in fact, as far as from London to

Moscow. You have altered the face of the war in a most remarkable way.

What it has meant in the skill and organization of movement and manoeuvres, what it has meant in the tireless endurance and self-denial of the troops and in the fearless leadership displayed in action, can be appreciated only by those who were actually on the spot. But I must tell you that the fame of the Desert Army has spread throughout the world.

After the surrender of Tobruk, there was a dark period when many people, not knowing us, not knowing the British and the nations of the British Empire, were ready to take a disparaging view. But now everywhere your work is spoken of with respect and admiration. When I was with the Chief of the Imperial General Staff at Casablanca and with the President of the United States, the arrival of the Desert Army in Tripoli was a new factor which influenced the course of our discussions and opened up hopeful vistas for the future. You are entitled to know these things, and to dwell upon them with that satisfaction which men in all modesty feel when a great work has been finally done. You have rendered a high service to your country and the common cause.

It must have been a tremendous experience driving forward day after day over this desert which it has taken me this morning more than six hours to fly at 200 miles an hour. You were pursuing a broken enemy, dragging on behind you this ever-lengthening line of communications, carrying the whole art of desert warfare to perfection. In the words of the old hymn, you have 'nightly pitched your moving tents a day's march nearer home.'

Yes, not only in the march of the army but in the progress of the war you have brought home nearer. I am here to thank you on behalf of His Majesty's Government of the British Isles and of all our friends the world over.

Hard struggles lie ahead. Rommel, the fugitive of Egypt, Cyrenaica and Tripolitania, in a non-stop race of 1,400 miles, is now trying to present himself as the deliverer of Tunisia. Along the eastern coast of Tunisia are large numbers of German and Italian troops, not yet equipped to their previous standard, but growing stronger. On the other side, another great operation, planned in conjunction with your advance, has carried the First British Army, our American comrades, and the French armies to within 30 or 40 miles of Bizerta and Tunis. Therefrom a military situation arises which everyone can understand.

The days of your victories are by no means at an end, and with forces which march from different quarters we may hope to achieve the final destruction or expulsion from the shores of Africa of every armed German or Italian. You must have felt relief when, after those many a hundred miles of desert, you came once more into a green land with trees and grass, and I do not think you will lose that advantage. As you go forward on further missions that will fall to your lot, you will fight in countries which will present undoubtedly serious tactical difficulties, but which none the less will not have that grim character of desert war which you have known how to endure and how to overcome.

Let me then assure you, soldiers and airmen, that your fellow-countrymen regard your joint work with admiration and gratitude, and that after the war when a man is asked what he did it will be quite sufficient for him to say, 'I marched and fought with the Desert Army.' And when history is written and all the facts are known, your feats will gleam and glow and will be a source of song and story long after we who are gathered here have passed away.

D-Day

6 June 1944

House of Commons

The House should, I think, take formal cognizance of the liberation of Rome by the Allied Armies under the command of General Alexander, with General Clark of the United States Service and General Oliver Leese in command of the Fifth and Eighth Armies respectively. This is a memorable and glorious event, which rewards the intense fighting of the last five months in Italy. . . .

I have also to announce to the House that during the night and the early hours of this morning the first of the series of landings in force upon the European Continent has taken place. In this case the liberating assault fell upon the coast of France. An immense armada of upwards of 4,000 ships, together with several thousand smaller craft, crossed the Channel. Massed airborne landings have been successfully effected behind the enemy lines, and landings on the beaches are proceeding at various points at the present time. The fire of the shore batteries has been largely quelled. The obstacles that were constructed in the sea have not proved so difficult as was apprehended. The Anglo-American Allies are sustained by about 11,000 first-line aircraft, which can be drawn upon as may be needed for the purposes of the battle. I cannot, of course, commit myself to any particular details. Reports are coming in in rapid succession. So far the commanders who are engaged report that everything is proceeding according to plan. And what a plan! This vast operation is undoubtedly the most complicated and difficult that has ever taken place. It involves tides, wind, waves, visibility, both from the air and the sea standpoint, and the combined employment of land, air and sea forces in the highest degree of intimacy and in contact with conditions which could not and cannot be fully foreseen.

There are already hopes that actual tactical surprise has been attained, and we hope to furnish the enemy with a succession of surprises during the course of the fighting. The battle that has now begun will grow constantly in scale and in intensity for many weeks to come, and I shall not attempt to speculate upon its course. This I may say, however. Complete unity prevails throughout the Allied Armies. There is a brotherhood in arms between us and our friends of the United States. There is complete confidence in the supreme commander, General Eisenhower, and his lieutenants, and also in the commander of the Expeditionary Force, General Montgomery. The ardour and spirit of the troops, as I saw myself, embarking in these last few days was splendid to witness.

'The price in blood . . . for the liberation of the soil of France'

28 September 1944

House of Commons

Churchill summarizes the progress of the Allied invasion.

Little more than seven weeks have passed since we rose for the summer vacation, but this short period has completely changed the face of the war in Europe. When we separated, the Anglo-American Armies were still penned in the narrow bridgehead and strip of coast from the base of the Cherbourg Peninsula to the approaches to Caen, which they had wrested from the enemy several weeks before. The Brest Peninsula was untaken, the German Army in the West was still hopeful of preventing us from striking out into the fields of France, the Battle of Normandy, which had been raging bloodily from the date of the landing, had not reached any decisive conclusion. What a transformation now meets our eyes! Not only Paris, but practically the whole of France, has been liberated as if by enchantment. Belgium has been rescued, part of Holland is already free, and the foul enemy, who for four years inflicted his cruelties and oppression upon these countries, has fled, losing perhaps 400,000 in killed and wounded, and leaving in our hands nearly half a million prisoners. Besides this, there may well be 200,000 cut off in the coastal fortresses or in Holland, whose destruction or capture may now be deemed highly probable. The Allied Armies have reached and in some places crossed the German frontier and the Siegfried Line.

All these operations have been conducted under the supreme command of General Eisenhower, and were the fruit of the world-famous battle of Normandy, the greatest and most decisive single battle of the entire war. Never has the exploitation of victory been carried to a higher perfection. The chaos and destruction wrought by the Allied Air Forces behind the battle front have been indescribable in narrative, and a factor of the utmost potency in the actual struggle. They have far surpassed, and reduce to petty dimensions, all that our army had to suffer from the German Air Force in 1940. Nevertheless, when we reflect upon the tremendous fire-power of modern weapons and the opportunity which they give for defensive and delaying action, we must feel astounded at the extraordinary speed with which the Allied Armies have advanced. The vast and brilliant encircling movement of the American Armies will ever be a model of military art, and an example of the propriety of running risks not only in the fighting – because most of the armies are ready to do that – but even more on the Q. side, or, as the Americans put it, the logistical side. It was with great pleasure that all of us saw the British and Canadian Armies, who had so long fought against heavy resistance by the enemy along the hinge of the Allied movement, show themselves also capable of lightning advances which have certainly not been surpassed anywhere.

Finally, by the largest airborne operation ever conceived or executed, a further all-important forward bound in the North has been achieved. Here I must pay a tribute, which the House will consider due, to the superb feat of arms performed by our First Airborne Division. Full and deeply moving accounts have already been given to the country and to the world of this glorious and fruitful operation, which will take a lasting place in our military annals, and will, in succeeding generations, inspire our youth with the highest ideals of duty and of daring. The cost has been heavy; the casualties in a single division have been grievous; but for those who mourn there is at least the consolation that the sacrifice was not needlessly demanded nor given without results. The delay caused to the enemy's advance upon Nijmegen enabled their British and American comrades in the other two airborne divisions, and the British Second Army, to secure intact the vitally important bridges and to form a strong bridgehead over the main stream of the Rhine at Nijmegen. 'Not in vain' may be the pride of those who have survived and the epitaph of those who fell.

To return to the main theme, Brest, Havre, Dieppe, Boulogne and Antwerp are already in our hands. All the Atlantic and Channel ports, from the Spanish frontier to the Hook of Holland, will presently be in our possession, yielding fine harbours and substantial masses of prisoners of war. All this has been accomplished by the joint exertions of the British and American Armies, assisted by the vehement and widespread uprising and fighting efforts of the French Maquis.

While this great operation has been taking its course,

an American and French landing on the Riviera coast, actively assisted by a British airborne brigade, a British Air Force, and the Royal Navy, has led with inconceivable rapidity to the capture of Toulon and Marseilles, to the freeing of the great strip of the Riviera coast, and to the successful advance of General Patch's Army up the Rhone Valley. This army, after taking over 80,000 prisoners, joined hands with General Eisenhower, and has passed under his command. When I had the opportunity on 15th August of watching – alas, from afar – the landing at Saint Tropez, it would have seemed audacious to hope for such swift and important results. They have, however, under the spell of the victories in the North, already been gained in super-abundance, and in less than half the time prescribed and expected in the plans which were prepared beforehand. So much for the fighting in France.

Simultaneously with that, very hard and successful fighting on a major scale has also proceeded on the Italian Front. General Alexander, who commands the armies in Italy with complete operational discretion, has under him the Fifth and Eighth Armies. The Fifth Army, half American and half British, with whom are serving the fine Brazilian Division, some of whose troops I had the opportunity of seeing – a magnificent band of men – is commanded by the United States General Clark, an officer of the highest quality and bearing, with a proud record of achievements behind him and his troops. The Eighth Army, under General Oliver Leese, whose qualities are also of the highest order, comprises the Polish Corps which fought so gallantly under General Anders, and a Greek Brigade which has already distinguished itself in the forefront of the battle. There is also fighting on this Front a strong force of Italians, who are ardent to free their country from the German grip and taint. This force will very soon be more than doubled in strength. The Lieutenant of the Realm is often with these troops.

The largest mass of all the troops on the Italian Front comes, of course, from the United Kingdom. Not far short of half the divisions on the whole front are from this Island. Joined with them are New Zealand, Canadian, South African and Indian Divisions, or perhaps I should say British-Indian Divisions, because, as is sometimes forgotten, one-third of them are British. The British Army in Italy includes also Palestinian units; and here I would mention the announcement, which I think will be appreciated and approved, that the Government have decided to accede to the request of the Jewish Agency for Palestine that a Jewish Brigade group should be formed to take part in active operations. I know there are vast numbers of Jews serving with our Forces and the American Forces throughout all the Armies, but it seems to me indeed appropriate that a special Jewish unit, a special unit of that race which has suffered indescribable torments from the Nazis, should be represented as a distinct formation amongst the forces gathered for their final overthrow, and I have no doubt they will not only take part in the struggle but also in the occupation which will follow.

A very hard task lies before the Army in Italy. It has already pierced at several points the strong Gothic line by which Kesselring has sought to defend the passage of the

Apennines. I had an opportunity of watching and following the advance of the Eighth Army across the Metauro River, which began on August 26th. The extraordinary defensive strength of the ground held by the enemy was obvious. The mountain ridges rise one behind the other in a seemingly endless succession, like the waves of the sea, and each had to be conquered or turned by superior force and superior weapons. The process was bound to be lengthy and costly, but it is being completed, has, in fact, been practically completed. At the same time, General Clark's Fifth Army, advancing from the Florence area, has pierced deep into the mountain ranges, and, having broken the enemy's centre, now stands on the northern slopes of the Apennines at no great distance from Bologna, a place of definite strategic importance. General Alexander has now definitely broken into the basin of the Po, but here we exchange the barriers of mountain ridges for the perpetual interruption of the ground by streams and canals. Nevertheless, conditions henceforward will be more favourable for the destruction or rout of Kesselring's Army, and this is the objective to which all British and Allied Forces will be unceasingly bent. Farther than that, it is not desirable to peer at the present moment.

I am now going to give a few facts and figures about the operations in Europe. These have been very carefully chosen to give as much information as possible to the House and to the public, while not telling the enemy anything he does not already know, or only telling him too late for it to be of any service to him. The speed with which the mighty British and American Armies in France were built up is almost incredible. In the first 24 hours a quarter of a million men were landed, in the teeth of fortified and violent opposition. By the 20th day a million men were ashore. There are now between two and three million men in France. Certainly the progress in the power of moving troops and landing troops has vastly increased since the early days, when we had to plunge into the war with no previous experience. But the actual number of soldiers was only part of the problem of transportation. These armies were equipped with the most perfect modern weapons and every imaginable contrivance of modern war, and an immense artillery supported all their operations. Enormous masses of armour of the highest quality and character gave them extraordinary offensive power and mobility. Many hundreds of thousands of vehicles sustained their movements, many millions of tons of stores have already been landed – the great bulk of everything over open beaches or through the synthetic harbours which I described when last I spoke to the House.

All this constitutes a feat of organization and efficiency which should excite the wonder and deserve the admiration of all military students, as well as the applause of the British and American nations and their Allies. I must pay my tribute to the United States Army, not only in their valiant and ruthless battleworthy qualities, but also in the skill of their commanders and the excellence of their supply arrangements. When one remembers that the United States four or five years ago was a peace-loving Power, without any great body of troops or munitions, and with only a very small regular Army to draw their commanders from, the American achievement is truly amazing.

After the intense training they have received for nearly three years, or more than three years in some cases, their divisions are now composed of regular professional soldiers whose military quality is out of all comparison with hurriedly raised wartime levies. These soldiers, like our own from Great Britain who have been even longer under arms, are capable of being placed immediately on landing in the battle line, and have proved themselves more than a match for the so-called veteran troops of Germany, who, though fighting desperately, are showing themselves decidedly the worse for wear. When I think of the measureless output of ships, munitions and supplies of all kinds with which the United States has equipped herself and has sustained all the fighting Allies in generous measure, and of the mighty war she is conducting, with troops of our Australian and New Zealand Dominions, over the spaces of the Pacific Ocean, this House may indeed salute our sister nation as being at the highest pinnacle of her power and fame.

I am very glad to say that we also have been able to make a worthy contribution. Some time ago, a statement was made by a Senator to the effect that the American public would be shocked to learn that they would have to provide 80 per cent of the forces to invade the Continent. I then said that at the outset of the invasion of France the British and American Forces would be practically equal, but that thereafter the American build-up would give them steadily the lead. I am glad to say that after 120 days of fighting we still bear, in the cross-Channel troops, a proportion of two to three in personnel and of four to five-and-a-half in fighting divisions in France. Casualties have followed very closely the proportions of the numbers. In fact, these troops fight so level that the casualties almost exactly follow the numbers engaged. We have, I regret to say, lost upwards of 90,000 men, killed, wounded and missing, and the United States, including General Patch's Army, over 145,000. Such is the price in blood paid by the English-speaking democracies for the actual liberation of the soil of France.

The Yalta Conference

27 February 1945

House of Commons

Churchill reports on the Yalta Conference.

The recent Conference of the three Powers in the Crimea faced realities and difficulties in so exceptional a manner that the result constituted an act of State, on which Parliament should formally express their opinion. His Majesty's Government feel they have the right to know where they stand with the House of Commons. A strong expression of support by the House will strengthen our position among our Allies. The intimate and sensitive connections between the Executive Government and the House of Commons will thereby also be made plain, thus showing the liveliness of our democratic institutions, and the subordination of Ministers to Parliamentary authority. The House will not shrink from its duty of pronouncing. We live in a time when equality of decision is required from all who take part in our public affairs. In this way also, the firm and tenacious character of the present Parliament, and, generally, of our Parliamentary institutions, emerging as they do fortified from the storms of the war, will be made manifest. We have therefore thought it right and necessary to place a positive Motion on the Paper, in support of which I should like to submit some facts and arguments to the House at the opening of this three days' Debate.

The difficulties of bringing about a Conference of the three heads of the Governments of the principal Allies are only too obvious. The fact that, in spite of all modern methods of communication, fourteen months elapsed between Teheran and Yalta is a measure of those difficulties. It is well known that His Majesty's Government greatly desired a triple meeting in the Autumn. We rejoiced when, at last, Yalta was fixed. On the way there, the British and United States delegations met at Malta to discuss the wide range of our joint military and political affairs. The combined Chiefs of Staff of the two countries were for three days in conference upon the great operations now developing on the Western Front, and upon the war plans against Japan, which it was appropriate for us to discuss together. The Foreign Secretary, accompanied by high officials and assistants, some of whom unhappily perished on the way, also met Mr Stettinius there. On the morning of 2nd February the cruiser which bore the President steamed majestically into the battle-scarred harbour. A plenary meeting of the combined Chiefs of Staff was held in the afternoon, at which the President and I approved the proposals which had been so carefully worked out in the preceding days for carrying our joint war effort to the highest pitch, and for the shaping and timing of the military operations . . .

After that, we all flew safely from Malta to the airfield in the Crimea, and motored over the mountains – about which very alarming accounts had been given, but these proved to be greatly exaggerated – until we found shelter on the Southern shore of the Crimea. This is protected by the mountains, and forms a beautiful Black Sea Riviera, where there still remain undestroyed by the Nazis a few villas and palaces of the vanished Imperial and aristocratic regime. By extreme exertions and every form of thoughtfulness and ingenuity, our Russian hosts had restored these dwellings to good order, and had provided for our accommodation and comfort in the true style of Russian hospitality. In the background were the precipices and the mountains; beyond them, the devastated fields and shattered dwellings of the Crimea, across which the armies have twice surged in deadly combat. Here on this shore, we laboured for nine days and grappled with many problems of war and policy while friendship grew. . . .

On world organization, there is little that I can say beyond what is contained in the Report of the Conference, and, of course, in the earlier reports which emanated from Dumbarton Oaks. In the Crimea, the three Great Powers agreed on a solution of the difficult question of voting procedure, to which no answer had been found at Dumbarton Oaks. Agreement on this vital matter has enabled us to take the next step forward in the setting-up of the new world organization, and the arrangements are in hand for the issue of invitations to the United Nations Conference which, as I have said, will meet in a couple of months at San Francisco. I wish I could give to the House full particulars of the solution of this question of the voting procedure, to which representatives of the three Great Powers, formerly in disagreement, have now wholeheartedly agreed. We thought it right, however, that we should consult both France and China, and should endeavour to secure their acceptance before the formula was published. For the moment, therefore, I can only deal with the matter in general terms.

Here is the difficulty which has to be faced. It is on the Great Powers that the chief burden of maintaining peace and security will fall. The new world organization must take into account this special responsibility of the Great Powers, and must be so framed as not to compromise their unity, or their capacity for effective action if it is called for at short notice. At the same time, the world organization cannot be based upon a dictatorship of the Great Powers. It is their duty to serve the world and not to rule it. We trust the voting procedure on which we agreed at Yalta meets these two essential points, and provides a system which is fair and acceptable, having regard to the evident difficulties, which will meet anyone who gives prolonged thought to the subject. . . .

The Crimea Conference leaves the Allies more closely united than ever before, both in the military and in the political sphere. Let Germany recognize that it is futile to hope for division among the Allies, and that nothing can avert her utter defeat. Further resistance will only be the cause of needless suffering. The Allies are resolved that Germany shall be totally disarmed, that Nazism and militarism in Germany shall be destroyed, that war criminals shall be justly and swiftly punished, that all German industry capable of military production shall be eliminated or controlled, and that Germany shall make compensation in kind to the utmost of her ability for damage done to Allied nations. On the other hand, it is not the purpose of the Allies to destroy the people of Germany, or leave them without the necessary means of subsistence. Our policy is not revenge; it is to take such measures as may be necessary to secure the future peace and safety of the world. There will be a place one day for Germans in the comity of nations, but only when all traces of Nazism and militarism have been effectively and finally extirpated. . . .

I now come to the most difficult and agitating part of the statement which I have to make to the House – the question of Poland. For more than a year past, and since the tide of war has turned so strongly against Germany, the Polish problem has been divided into two main issues – the frontiers of Poland and the freedom of Poland.

The House is well aware from the speeches I have made to them that the freedom, independence, integrity and sovereignty of Poland have always seemed to His Majesty's Government more important than the actual frontiers. To establish a free Polish nation with a good home to live in has always far outweighed, in my mind, the actual tracing of the frontier line, or whether these boundaries should be shifted on both sides of Poland farther to the West. . . .

But even more important than the frontiers of Poland, within the limits now disclosed, is the freedom of Poland. The home of the Poles is settled. Are they to be masters in their own house? Are they to be free, as we in Britain and the United States or France are free? Is their sovereignty and their independence to be untrammelled, or are they to become a mere projection of the Soviet State, forced against their will, by an armed minority, to adopt a Communist or totalitarian system? Well, I am putting the case in all its bluntness. It is a touchstone far more sensitive and vital than the drawing of frontier lines. Where does Poland stand? Where do we all stand on this?

Most solemn declarations have been made by Marshal Stalin and the Soviet Union that the sovereign independence of Poland is to be maintained, and this decision is now joined in both by Great Britain and the United States. Here also, the world organization will in due course assume a measure of responsibility. The Poles will have their future in their own hands, with the single limitation that they must honestly follow, in harmony with their Allies, a policy friendly to Russia. That is surely reasonable.

The procedure which the three Great Powers have unitedly adopted to achieve this vital aim is set forth in unmistakable terms in the Crimea declaration. The agreement provides for consultations, with a view to the establishment in Poland of a new Polish Provisional Government of National Unity, with which the three major Powers can all enter into diplomatic relations, instead of some recognizing one Polish Government and the rest another, a situation which, if it had survived the Yalta Conference, would have proclaimed to the world disunity and confusion. We had to settle it, and we settled it there. No binding restrictions have been imposed upon the scope and method of those consultations. His Majesty's Government intend to do all in their power to ensure that they shall be as wide as possible, and that representative Poles of all democratic parties are given full freedom to come and make their views known. Arrangements for this are now being made in Moscow by the Commission of three, comprising M. Molotov, and Mr Harriman and Sir Archibald Clark Kerr, representing the United States and Great Britain respectively. It will be for the Poles themselves, with such assistance as the Allies are able to give them, to agree upon the composition and constitution of the new Polish Government of National Unity. Thereafter, His Majesty's Government, through their representative in Poland, will use all their influence to ensure that the free elections to which the new Polish Government will be pledged shall be fairly carried out under all proper democratic safeguards.

Our two guiding principles in dealing with all these problems of the Continent and of liberated countries, have been clear: While the war is on, we give help to anyone who can kill a Hun; when the war is over, we look to the solution of a free, unfettered, democratic election. Those are the two principles which this Coalition Government have applied, to the best of their ability, to the circumstances and situations in this entangled and infinitely varied development. . . .

The House should read carefully again and again – those Members who have doubts – the words and the terms of the Declaration, every word of which was the subject of the most profound and searching attention by the Heads of the three Governments, and by the Foreign Secretaries and all their experts. How will this Declaration be carried out? How will phrases like 'Free and unfettered elections on the basis of universal suffrage and secret ballot' be interpreted? Will the 'new' Government be 'properly' constituted, with a fair representation of the Polish people, as far as can be made practicable at the moment, and as soon as possible? Will the elections be free and unfettered? Will the candidates of all democratic parties be able to present themselves to the electors, and to conduct their campaigns? What are democratic parties? People always take different views. Even in our own country there has been from time to time an effort by one party or the other to claim that they are the true democratic party, and the rest are either Bolsheviks or Tory landlords. What are democratic parties? Obviously, this is capable of being settled. Will the election be what we should say was fair and free in this country, making some allowance for the great confusion and disorder which prevails? There are a great number of parties in Poland. We have agreed that all those that are democratic parties – not Nazi or Fascist parties or parties of collaborators with the enemy – all these will be able to take their part.

These are questions upon which we have the clearest views, in accordance with the principles of the Declaration on liberated Europe, to which all three Governments have duly subscribed. It is on that basis that the Moscow Commission of three was intended to work, and on that basis it has already begun to work.

The impression I brought back from the Crimea, and from all my other contacts, is that Marshal Stalin and the Soviet leaders wish to live in honourable friendship and equality with the Western democracies. I feel also that their word is their bond. I know of no Government which stands to its obligations, even in its own despite, more solidly than the Russian Soviet Government. I decline absolutely to embark here on a discussion about Russian good faith. It is quite evident that these matters touch the whole future of the world. Sombre indeed would be the fortunes of mankind if some awful schism arose between the Western democracies and the Russian Soviet Union, if the future world organization were rent asunder, and if new cataclysms of inconceivable violence destroyed all that is left of the treasures and liberties of mankind.

'This is your victory'

8 May 1945

Balcony of the Ministry
of Health, London

In the face of enormous celebrating crowds blocking Whitehall, Churchill gave this speech. When he declared: 'This is your victory', the crowd roared back: 'No – it is yours.'

God bless you all. This is your victory! It is the victory of the cause of freedom in every land. In all our long history we have never seen a greater day than this. Everyone, man or woman, has done their best. Everyone has tried. Neither the long years, nor the dangers, nor the fierce attacks of the enemy, have in any way weakened the independent resolve of the British nation. . . .

My dear friends, this is your hour. This is not victory of a party or of any class. It's a victory of the great British nation as a whole. We were the first, in this ancient island, to draw the sword against tyranny. After a while we were left all alone against the most tremendous military power that has been seen. We were all alone for a whole year.

There we stood, alone. Did anyone want to give in? [The crowd shouted 'No.'] Were we down-hearted? ['No!']

The lights went out and the bombs came down. But every man, woman and child in the country had no thought of quitting the struggle. London can take it. So we came back after long months from the jaws of death, out of the mouth of hell, while all the world wondered. When shall the reputation and faith of this generation of English men and women fail? I say that in the long years to come not only will the people of this island but of the world, whenever the bird of freedom chirps in human hearts, look back to what we've done and they will say 'Do not despair, do not yield to violence and tyranny, march straight forward and die if need be – unconquered.' Now we have emerged from one deadly struggle – a terrible foe has been cast on the ground and awaits our judgment and our mercy.

But there is another foe who occupies large portions of the British Empire, a foe stained with cruelty and greed – the Japanese. I rejoice we can all take a night off today and another day tomorrow. Tomorrow our great Russian allies will also be celebrating victory and after that we must begin the task of rebuilding our health and homes, doing our utmost to make this country a land in which all have a chance, in which all have a duty, and we must turn ourselves to fulfil our duty to our own countrymen, and to our gallant allies of the United States who were so foully and treacherously attacked by Japan. We will go hand in hand with them. Even if it is a hard struggle we will not be the ones who will fail.